Cheech & Chong's
ALMOST LEGAL

BOOK FOR
STONERS

Cheech & Chong's ALMOST LEGAL BOOK FOR STONERS

By **CHEECH MARIN** and **TOMMY CHONG**
with **GREG JONES**

RUNNING PRESS
PHILADELPHIA · LONDON

Books published by Running Press are available at special discounts for bulk purchases in the
United States by corporations, institutions, and other organizations. For more information,
please contact the Special Markets Department at the Perseus Books Group, 2300 Chestnut
Street, Suite 200, Philadelphia, PA 19103, or call (800) 810-4145, ext. 5000, or e-mail special.
markets@perseusbooks.com.

ISBN 978-0-7624-4987-3
Library of Congress Control Number: 2013943533

E-book ISBN 978-0-7624-4988-0

9   8   7   6   5   4   3   2   1
Digit on the right indicates the number of this printing

Cover and interior design by Susan Van Horn
Edited by Jennifer Kasius
Photo research by Susan Oyama
Typography: Eclyptica, Excelsior, Funkydori, GothamNarrow,
John Lennon, Social Gothic, and Tutti Paffuti

This book is a work of entertainment and information only, and is in no way
meant to encourage readers to engage in illegal activity.

Running Press Book Publishers
2300 Chestnut Street
Philadelphia, PA 19103-4371

Visit us on the web!
www.runningpress.com

This book is dedicated to all the
stoners out there—may all of your
cares go up in smoke.

Contents

THIS IS THE BOOK
You Wish You Had
AND NOW HAVE

You know man, we never had a book like this back in the day. Back when everyone wore tie dye and bellbottoms and had roach clips with feathers hanging down from the rearview mirrors of their '57 Chevys, when bongs and joints and soda cans with pinhole bowls sat on stoners' wooden-crate coffee tables and grass only came in a few different flavors like Acapulco Gold and California sensimilla and Jamaican and Hawaiian and Thai Stick. We can't get those days back, and sometimes we can't even remember them. And that's why we decided to put this book together.

Stonerhood is all about friends and relaxation and mind expansion and fun, and stoners will enjoy learning the best way to improvise a pipe as much as reading about the real story behind "420." You'll hear what wise people from past and present have to say about the magic plant, and get turned on to hundreds of classic stoner ideas and activities.

Not sure how to go about getting a bag of bud? We'll tell you what to expect from the average dealer, and other ways to score.

Not convinced that marijuana is the least harmful pastime compared to alcohol, cigarettes, and every other mind-altering drug? We'll prove beyond the shadow of a bong that it's true.

Need to bone up on how cannabis became illegal, why it's still illegal, and what you can do to help make it legal again? Read on.

Feeling isolated because you can't find other folks like you, who enjoy partaking in one of God's greatest gifts to mankind? The reality is, there are many stoners right in your neighborhood—you just need to brush up on the signs that say, "I'm cool." And we got that covered.

We also name the different strains of weed available today, describe how to make a stash kit, turn you on to freaky smoking games and tricks, give some love to all the dedicated activists who are fighting to "legalize it," and give props to the great cannabis festivals held around the world each year. And here and there, we throw in other random stuff just to keep you on your toes. We have some fun with stoner stereotypes, and dig up and dish out some serious information you probably haven't heard before.

And whoever and whatever we forget to include in this book, we can always make up for it in *Cheech and Chong's Next Book for Stoners.*

The thing about stonerhood is that it's always been about the people. And that's what this book is about—the places stoners go, the things stoners say and do, and the stuff that stoners like, plus games and doodling and other trippy activities, too.

But you know the main reason why we wrote this book?

Because marijuana is a good thing.

There, we said it. It's something every stoner—millions of them—have great memories of throughout their life, even if they've forgotten some of them. From the first time you smoked Thai stick out of an apple core at the drive-in movie theater in high school, to the white widow hit you vaporized this morning, the stoner life is something to be proud of and to celebrate and to share and to learn all about.

So sit back, light up, and tune in.

And one last thing . . . has anyone seen the lighter?

BECAUSE MARIJUANA IS A GOOD THING.

THE DOPE ON WEED

A Brief History of Cannabis from 10,000 BC until Last December

THE EARLY DAYS

Once upon a time, approximately a lot of years ago, a seed fell into the ground and a brand new kind of plant started to grow. The leaves came out all bright green and long and pointy and they had these really cool serrated edges and they smelled real nice. And once the plant grew to be real tall, all the green and purple and red leaves started curling together into little leaf balls, and sugary crystals formed on those balls. And it was a good thing, even though you don't usually want anything growing on your balls.

Today we know this plant by the manmade scientific name, *Cannabis sativa*—or just cannabis. We also call it other things, like marijuana, hemp, weed, grass, Mary Jane, bhang, bud, ganja, bamba, ace, 420, herb, kif, tea, or some other code word that one of your friends invented so narcs wouldn't know what you're talking about. There are lots more other names for our favorite plant, but we'll get to that later.

Nobody knows for sure when humans first used the cannabis plant, whether you're talking about the "hemp" plant that doesn't get you high, or the "marijuana" plant, which does get you high, assuming you're holding.

But as far as evidence goes, archaeologists have dug up artifacts from people who used hemp fibers as long ago as 10,000 BC in China. And the first known use of cannabis seeds for food and oil is also on record in China, going all the way back to 6000 BC. They've found shoes, fabric, clothes, rope, bowstrings for weapons, mats, and more in digs dating back to before the Common Era. In fact, the plant was so important to Chinese culture for so long, they called their country "the land of mulberry and hemp."

The earliest evidence of people using cannabis to get "high" is a bowl with charred cannabis seeds dating to around 3000 BC that was found by archaeologists in present-day Romania. And the oldest evidence in China was found inside the tomb of a Chinese shaman, dating to around 800 BC. There were a couple of vessels filled with almost two pounds of THC-laden cannabis.

By that time, humans all over the world were using cannabis for making rope, fabric, and many other necessities, using its seeds, oils, and stalks for food, fuel, and fiber, and eventually, fun.

THE PAPER SITUATION

One of the most important inventions that people ever invented is paper. And the world's first known paper was made with hemp fibers, around 110 BC, in China. Before paper, everything that people wanted to write down had to be written on expensive silk or, more commonly, carved onto tablets made out of clay or rock or wood or other bulky stuff. It took a long time to write anything down, and an even longer time to carry whatever was written down from here to there. So knowledge moved around the world very very very slowly, kind of like today for anyone still using dial-up.

According to Chinese legend, modern paper-making was invented by a court official named Ts'ai Lun in 105 AD. One day, so to speak, he woke up, crushed a pile of hemp fibers and mulberry bark etc. into pulp form, let it sit in water until the fibers rose up to the top all tangled together, then moved the mash from the water to a mold, and when the fiber dried together in the mold it formed a sheet that could be written on. Paper!

So he took the newly invented paper to the emperor, thinking he would treat him like a hero with a parade, concubines, and a lifetime supply of rice. But there were doubters. Legend says that in order to turn the naysayers around, Ts'ai Lun did something crazy to prove a point

Papermaking, China

about the power of paper. With a little help from some friends, he faked his death and was buried alive in a coffin with a paper lid. His buddies told the mourners that if the paper lid of the coffin burned, Ts'ai Lun would rise from the dead. The paper did burn, and Ts'ai Lun leapt up out of the coffin and scared the crap out of everyone.

The people thought the whole thing was miraculous, and acknowledged the power of paper.

To this day, the Chinese continue the custom of burning paper over the tombs of their deceased loved ones.

Any way you fold it, it was an awesome invention, so awesome that the xenophobic Chinese (have you seen that Wall?) kept it to themselves for hundreds of years, until the ninth century when some Arab soldiers captured some Chinese prisoners who were "holding" (paper, that is) during the Battle of Samarkand, in land that is now Russia. In what might be the world's first case of mail fraud, the Arabs stole the papers, and later somehow figured out how to deconstruct it and then reconstruct it and then trade it for everything from camels to coconuts. In other words, paper-making soon went global and led to a huge increase in knowledge everywhere, and a growing importance for cannabis.

HIGH AND HEALTHY

Once cannabis started to get discovered and traded around the world outside China—between 1200 and 800 BC—people everywhere started getting high as a kite. (Coincidentally, for fans of idioms, the kite was invented in 800 BC.)

According to the earliest-known archaeological finds, followers of Taoism—a back-to-nature philosophy—figured out how to use cannabis for intoxication. Soon after that, the squares of Chinese society who were threatened by the laid-back Taoists voiced their disapproval and began condemning the recreational and spiritual use of cannabis. Sound familiar?

But despite people of all eras attacking cannabis, many others have embraced the plant for its high and for its health benefits for thousands of years, everywhere:

1200 BC
Cannabis is referenced in the sacred Hindu text Atharvaveda as "Sacred Grass," one of the five sacred plants of India, and is used as medicine and in ritual offerings to Shiva.

700 BC
The Zoroastrian Zend-Avesta refers to cannabis as a "good narcotic."

700 BC
Scythian tribes in modern-day Iran place cannabis seeds in royal tombs.

500 BC
Cannabis is brought to northern Europe—the future home of Amsterdam—by the Scythians.

70
Greek physician Dioscorides mentions the medicinal use of cannabis.

100
Gold and glass-paste stash boxes for storing cannabis dating from this period are found by archaeologists.

170
Roman physician Galen writes about the psychoactive use of cannabis.

Dioscorides, Greek physician and pharmacologist

FROM LEFT: Marco Polo • India, smoking Hookah

500
The Jewish Talmud refers to the euphoric aspects of cannabis.

900
The use of cannabis-based hashish spreads throughout Arabia.

1155
Narratives from this time in Persia discuss Sufi master Sheik Haidar's use of cannabis to get high.

1271
Marco Polo tells stories of Asian cannabis use to Europeans.

1300s
Ibn al-Baytar of Spain describes the psychoactive use of cannabis.

1300s
Arab traders bring cannabis to the East Coast of Africa.

1700s
Cannabis use spreads across Constantinople in modern-day Turkey.

1840
Medicinal preparations using cannabis are available in America.

1843
The "Hashish Eater's Club" is established in Paris.

1856
British tax the trade of cannabis in India.

1890
The Greek government prohibits the use of cannabis.

1890
Cannabis becomes illegal in Turkey.

1894
The British government issues the India Hemp Drugs Commission Report. Among other findings, it concludes that recreational use of cannabis produces no injurious effects on humans.

1890s
Approximately 80,000 kg of cannabis is imported into India from Central Asia each year.

1915-1927
Recreational use of cannabis prohibited in California (1915), Texas (1919), Louisiana (1924), and New York (1927).

1926
Cannabis is prohibited in Lebanon.

1928
Recreational use of cannabis is banned in Britain.

1934-1935
Chinese government begins banning cannabis cultivation in several regions.

1937
The U.S. government passes the Marijuana Tax Act to make production and use of cannabis a federal crime.

FROM LEFT: Coffee Shop, Amsterdam • Marijuana legalized in Washington State

1970s
The cannabis coffee-shop phenomenon begins in Amsterdam.

1972
The Nixon administration in the U.S. urges that the use of cannabis be legalized, but the recommendation is ignored by Congress.

1973
Afghanistan makes cannabis production and use illegal.

1973
Oregon decriminalizes marijuana to a "violation" which is less severe than a felony or misdemeanor.

1975
The U.S. Food and Drug Administration establishes the "Compassionate Use" program for medical marijuana.

1975
California, Alaska, Ohio, and Colorado decriminalize marijuana.

1978
New York, Mississippi, Nebraska, and North Carolina decriminalize marijuana.

1988
U.S. Drug Enforcement Agency Judge Francis Young finds that marijuana has beneficial medical use and should be reclassified as a prescriptive drug. Congress takes no action.

2008
Massachusetts passed a vote initiative to decriminalize possession of up to one ounce, punishable by a $100 fine.

2012
Voters in Colorado and Washington unanimously pass laws that will legalize marijuana for recreational use.

December 6, 2012
Recreational use of marijuana becomes legal in Washington state, U.S.A.

The Future
The history of cannabis is still being written, and stoners everywhere hope the trail blazed by Washingtonians and Coloradoans will soon be followed by all other Americans to legalize responsible recreational use of marijuana and industrial use of hemp throughout the United States. And then the rest of the world.

You gotta hand it to the stoners who put bumper stickers on their cars saying what's up to the world. Just don't ask them to smoke you up when they pick you up; they probably shouldn't be holding when driving with these kinds of pot-friendly messages on the bumper.

I BREAK FOR BUD

PRO CHOICE

HONK FOR HEMP! HONK FOR HEMP!

Dave Was Here

LEGALIZE IT!

WAKEY BAKEY

How to SCORE

Marijuana grows like a weed almost anywhere—north, south, east, west, in fields and greenhouses, labs and garages, basements and spare bedrooms, closets and crawlspaces, and even in little backyard gardens.

So it should be really easy to score some grass whenever you need it, right?

Wrong, man.

Until it becomes legal all over and corner stores are selling packs of Marlbojuana cigarettes, stoners have to stay crafty and use all means to feed their jones for weed.

Your Dealer

The dealer has been the main vein of stoner culture for decades. He gets the stuff in bales from the growers, puts it in bags for the stoners, and often smokes you up as a bonus. He typically stays up late, sleeps in late, and gets you your weed later than promised and usually due to hazy circumstances. But you always let him slide and come back for more—what else can you do? Broken promises, mysterious delays, communication breakdowns, and the occasional shitty shit are all part of the drill. If you've been a stoner for a while, you recall being run through the mill yourself.

PHONE CALL TO DEALER DAVE

DAVE: Hello?

YOU: Hey man, it's Hugh.

DAVE: Hugh?

YOU: Yeah, man, Hugh, from the apartment over the bakery.

DAVE: The bakery?

YOU: Yeah, the bakery, near the fire hou—

DAVE: Fire?!!!

YOU: No, man, there's no fire. I live near the fire house. . .

DAVE: Oh, okay. Right, Hugh! What's up, man?

YOU: I was just wondering, "Anything going on?"

DAVE: No, man, not really.

YOU: *[Muffled curse.]*

DAVE: I'm just sitting here watching TV.

YOU: So . . . nothing's "going on"? You have nothing?

DAVE: Ohhhh. No! I mean, yeah! I mean, I have something. I'm just doing nothing. Whaddya need?

YOU: Cool. I wanna get, uh . . . one.

DAVE: One lid?

YOU: Um, ye-yeah. One lid, I mean, you know, one hat.

DAVE: One hat? *[Thinks for a second.]* Ohhhh, right. One hat. *[Laughs.]* Why don't you come over.

YOU: All right! I'll be over in a couple hours, at, like, seven.

DAVE: Well hurry up, because I only have one lid—I mean, hat—left *[laughs]*.

YOU: In that case, I'll be right over. Hold it for me, ok?

DAVE: Sure man, I'll wear it till you get here. *[Laughs hysterically, hanging up.]*

You grab your wallet and car keys and run out the door. You drive as fast as you can across town to Dave's house, over the speed limit the whole way, and get there in twenty minutes.

You park down the block, walk nonchalantly toward Dave's house (while scanning every car and tree and trash can and window for the man) then turn into the driveway and quickly step to the side door that leads to Dave's basement apartment.

You knock. You knock again. One more time now. You look through the little door window but can't see through the tie-dyed curtain. He's gotta be here! You kneel down and look through the living-room window, and see Dave sitting on the couch watching TV. You tap on the window, and in slow motion, Dave turns and looks at you. He waves, and turns back around. You keep looking at him. Twenty seconds later, you tap again, and Dave turns in slow motion and looks at you. This time, he smiles, stands up, comes to the door and lets you in.

DAVE: Hey man, how you doing?

YOU: What's up, dude? You got my hat?
 [You laugh.]

DAVE: Hat? *[Looks confused.]*

YOU: Yeah man, my lid.

DAVE: Oh, right! *[Laughs hysterically.]* Your hat! *[Continues laughing hysterically.]*

YOU: *[Smiling, patiently.]* That's right. Is it good stuff?

DAVE: What stuff?

YOU: The stuff. The lid, man.

DAVE: The lid? I only had one lid left, man, and I sold it to a guy like ten minutes ago. You should have come by earlier.

YOU: But I just called you twenty minutes ago!

DAVE: Oh man, that was you? Then who was that other guy?

YOU: *[Fuming, patiently.]* So . . . you got no more lids?

DAVE: Nah, man. Sorry.

YOU: Fuck! Oh, well, call me when you get some more, ok?

DAVE: Yeah, okay man, I will.

[You walk through the door and Dave closes it; then opens it again.]

DAVE: If you want, man, I can sell you a half a lid. . . .

YOU: You do have some?

DAVE: Sure, yeah. I just don't have any more full lids. You wanted a lid, right?

YOU: Well, I wanted—

DAVE: A hat, right? *[Laughs hysterically.]*

YOU: I'll take anything.

DAVE: Well all I have are a bunch of nickels and dimes and halfs.

YOU: Tell you what, man. Give me two eights, one quarter, and one half.

DAVE: Cool, man. Doin' your Christmas shopping early, huh? [Laughs.]

YOU: *[Exasperated.]* Exactly, Dave.

Your Roommate

If you're lucky you'll have a cool roommate with a two-way understanding that *mi ganja es su ganja*. So when you're dry, you'll know it's okay to cop a bud from your bud until you can get your own bag to share.

But what if your roomie is out of the house and not answering his phone, text, or email?

If he hasn't told you his secret stash place, you'll just have to find it, most likely in one of these popular hiding spots:

1. Guitar case
2. Underwear drawer
3. Fish tank
4. Speakers
5. Amps
6. Under mattress
7. Pillow
8. Shirt pocket
9. Laundry hamper
10. Notebook
11. Fridge
12. Behind poster
13. Cigar box
14. Bible

420 Delivery Services

We never got this kind of service back in the day, but in the last fifteen years or so, stoners in big cities (and some smaller ones) have enjoyed the services of highly professional marijuana delivery companies that seem to operate like corporations.

The way it works is genius. New customers get referred by an existing customer, and then they get a membership number and their contact info goes into the service's computer database. When you call the service, they know who you are and where you are, and a courier arrives within thirty minutes—typically on a bicycle with a backpack. (If you time it right, you can call the pizza place and have the pot and the pizza get there one after the other.)

When the courier arrives, looking mighty hip and typically blazed, they pull a box out of their backpack containing dozens of little clear acrylic cubes filled with several grams of each kind of bud, with white-tape labels describing the strain. The couriers always know a lot about what they're holding, and can give you tips and buying advice like any professional sommelier might do with fine wines in a fancy restaurant. The costs are always higher with delivery services than other dealers and friend connections, but the quality is always top-notch and the convenience is unmatched.

Surprisingly, there are several of these delivery services in almost every major city, and they generally operate without getting busted. Except for one of the more famous services—famous because it did get busted and exposed. The "Cartoon Network" (no connection to the TV network!) in New York City had a database of 50,000 customers and got 600 calls per day!

Join a Doobie Session

No one's a stranger among stoners, since all stoners find themselves in need of a shared doobie sometimes, and have no problem extending their own J to others in need whenever and wherever. But there is an art to getting into the circle, and the different scenarios call for different steps that could lead to new friends—and a whole new outlook on the day.

AT a CONCERT

If you're seeing a stoner band or musician, like Santana, the Dead, Pink Floyd, Neil Young, the Banana Splits, etc., you may not have to ask anyone to turn you on—the contact buzz from the air in the audience might be enough to get you as high as Neil Young's falsetto.

But if you're not catching a contact buzz, you'll have to do a little pot-reconnaissance to find the direct source of smoke and hopefully join the session.

At most concerts of a certain genre, there will be someone lighting up to your left, or your right, or your front, or your back—or all of the above.

First thing to do is to look around and make a mental note of where the narcs—or rent-a-cops—are standing. The good thing is, they usually wear bright yellow "Security" shirts, and since no one else ever wears yellow, they're easy to spot.

Next, scan the areas around you on all sides, looking for the telltale signs of a group of stoners in action:

One person's head in a group is leaning forward and down (they're trying to keep the lighter flame from being spotted by narcs)

There's a brief flash of fire from a lighter (a sustained flame of light just means an audience member is requesting that the band play "Freebird").

Other people outside the session are sneaking looks over at the group and elbowing their friends to look too (notice if these onlookers begin to drool).

When you identify the closest group of 420 friends, you've done about 99 percent of the work. You then just have to walk over to the session, stand next to the last person, and when the joint or bowl comes to them, tap their arm and give them a nod along with a pleading, begging, beseeching type of look on your face. If the last person in the group is like ninety-five percent of stoners, the doobie will be in your fingers in a flash.

Just do a quick puff, puff, pass, say "Thanks," and split.

ON a COLLEGE CAMPUS

This is probably the best place to jump into a smoking session.

Since you will most likely already be drunk, there's no need to suggest that you act with any discretion. And you don't even need to identify the stoners. Just walk into any gathering—excluding gatherings like Math Club or the Young Republicans—and blurt out, "Anyone got any weed? Who can spark one up for me? I need to get hiiiighhh! Anybody gonna hook me up? Yeeeoww!!"

At most colleges, you won't even have to ask twice before someone (or two or three) pulls out a blunt or a bag or a vaporizer and obliges.

IN A PARK

What's better than a nice stroll through a beautiful park on a gorgeous summer afternoon with the breeze blowing, birds chirping, and chippies flaunting their beautiful bodies? How about catching a nice broccoli buzz while strolling through a beautiful park on a gorgeous summer afternoon with the breeze blowing, birds chirping, and chippies flaunting their beautiful bodies?

But if your baggie is empty, the only thing buzzing will be the bees if you don't find some hip friends, fast.

It's easy to spot the spliffers in a park. Sitting close together: check. Passing something back and forth: check. Wafts of smoke swirling into the blue sky above them: check. Happy little smiles on their faces: check.

You really don't want to walk right up to these people. Odds are, they'll think you're a narc and all kinds of craziness will ensue. One of them will quickly eat the joint, burning their tongue and esophagus in the process. One of them will get up and run into the woods. And one of them will take two steps to the left, sit down, face the other direction, and before you even speak, will proclaim that they've never met the other two in their entire life.

Don't be a buzzkill.

Instead, ask the guys across the park with the Frisbee or hacky sack if you can join in the game. (But first, ask them if they have any ganja to share. If they don't, continue reading.) Then gradually start moving the game closer to the tokers. By the time you get close enough to accidentally toss the Frisbee or hacky sack onto their blanket, they'll already know what you're doing and will offer you a toke with their left hand while returning your toy with their right.

AT A PARTY

If you are at a mixed party, where some do and some don't, it's gonna take a little bit of work to find out who does and who doesn't. Normally you don't want to ask just anyone if they're holding or if they know who is—you don't want to offend someone who doesn't do the doob by insinuating that they do do it by asking if they do, do you?

Your best bet is to make some observations, and ask some innocent-sounding questions, to root out the likeminded—and hopefully the likeminded is holding.

Turn to page 115 to get the 4-1-1 on who's 420-friendly.

Forgotten Hidden Stashes

Most stoners always stash away a bud or two when they make a score. You just tuck it away somewhere hidden, and when the rest of the stuff gets all used up, you got something to bust out. Problem is, stoners often forget where they stash their stashes! If this happens to you, here are all the places you should look for your forgotten hidden stashes:

1. Guitar case
2. Underwear drawer
3. Fish tank
4. Speakers
5. Amps
6. Under mattress
7. Pillow
8. Shirt pocket
9. Laundry hamper
10. Notebook
11. Fridge
12. Behind poster
13. Cigar box
14. Bible

PROS

Like everything else, marijuana has its good stuff and its bad stuff. So we sat down on a couch one night and wrote down a list including just a very small per-centage of all the good things, and literally all of the bad things.

Taps into universal love

Helps win gold medals

Makes you laugh, and laughing is healthy

Inspires hit songs

Your friends are funnier

Fends off depression

Puts things in perspective

Reveals truths about architecture

Promotes sharing

Makes getting out of bed easier

Is NOT addictive

Making friends was never so easy

Movies are funnier

Reduces anger

Puts you in tune with your body

Teaches the metric system

Taps into universal understanding

You're supporting America's #1 crop

Makes you feel high

Dogs are funnier

Sleeping is easier

Causes permasmile

Makes masturbation more fun

Reveals the BS in many things

Inspires great music

It evens you out

Makes other people more interesting

Reveals truths about the engineering behind the folding table in the corner

Inspires great art

It's a great teacher

Food tastes better

Raises your melatonin level A LOT

Sitcoms are funnier

Makes sex more fun

Melts away frustration

Excellent replacement for pharmaceuticals

Makes physical activity more interesting

Inspires new snack combinations

Opens your mind

Enhances meditation

Lots of medical studies prove it's safe

Games are more fun

Reveals truths about politicians

Does NOT cause cancer

Always provides a discovery of some sort

Discourages violence

Walking your dog is more fun

Makes you one with nature

Makes you one with your couch

Prevents migraines

Promotes soul-searching

Reveals truths about how to achieve world peace

Makes you want to invent stuff

Removes all doubt about the existence of extraterrestrials

Fox News is funnier

Promotes sanity

Helps you realize how incredibly cool cats are

Does NOT cause emphysema

Songs are more meaningful

Inspires big ideas

Makes a walk around the block an adventure

Doesn't hurt anyone

Makes you love everything

Better than alcohol for many reasons

Makes anything more interesting

Relieves all kinds of pains

You are funnier

Inspires you to rethink your life—in a good way

Stressbuster

Slows down the world

Twenty million people world-wide do it every day

Fights against hardened arteries: Fact

Makes sports more fun

Reveals truths about why turtles have shells

Pauly Shore is funnier

Inspires deep thinking

Ordinary words are funnier

Turns strangers into friends

Makes a hot shower a religious experience

Inspires creative guitar playing

Aquariums are more interesting

Reveals truths about your cat

Everything is funnier

It just plain feels good

and CONS

IT'S ILLEGAL

Destroying Marijuana plants, Chicago, 1958

How a Plant Became Illegal

Murderers, burglars, rapists, crooked G-men, Bernie Madoff . . . now those are criminals. But for the police to take a guy or girl who's holding a bag of leaves and throw them in jail, confiscate their property, take them away from family, ruin their reputation, destroy their financial stability, and basically kill their buzz . . . now that's just fucked up.

The question is, how did the dudes in the government ever pass a law to make a naturally occurring plant illegal? (Do you think money might be involved? Hmmm.)

First of all, you need to know what hemp and cannabis were up to before becoming illegal in the USA. . . .

The Good Times

Archaeologists know that cannabis was among the first crops cultivated by human beings, around 12,000 years ago, helping to shift from hunter-gatherers to agricultural communities and the birth of civilization.

Cannabis has always been one of the planet's largest agricultural crops, leading to thousands of products and enterprises, and producing the majority of the world's fiber, fabric, lighting oil, paper, and medicines.

For thousands of years, cannabis was the most widely used medicine in the world, truly helping tens of millions of people handle the pain and discomfort of multiple illnesses and injuries, with virtually no harmful side effects.

We already know that the first paper on Earth was made from hemp. In America, Benjamin Franklin started one of the first paper mills and the first printing press, using hemp fiber for paper which freed the young country from England's tyrannical control of paper and printing—a huge step toward independence.

George Washington and Thomas Jefferson, two of America's greatest founding fathers, both grew hemp on their farms and were outspoken in their praise for the plant's importance to America.

The first American flag was made with hemp fiber.

The draft of the Declaration of Independence that was released on July 4, 1776—the document that established the United States of America—was written on hemp paper.

Henry Ford's first Model-T car was built to run on hemp gasoline, and it was actually constructed from hemp—its hemp-plastic panels had an impact strength that was ten times stronger than steel.

Early twentieth-century government studies found that one acre of hemp equals about four acres of trees, in terms of paper production. And it takes less shit (that's fertilizer, to you) to grow! In 1916, the U.S. government stated that by the 1940s all paper would come from hemp and that no more trees needed to be cut down for paper. In fact, plans were in the works to implement hemp production for paper programs. . . .

But something bad happened along the way.

Crop Killers

The current federal U.S. law criminalizing the cultivation and possession of cannabis (both marijuana and hemp) can be directly attributed to three men—Henry J. Anslinger, Lammont DuPont, and William Randolph Hearst.

Anslinger was appointed the head of the Federal Bureau of Narcotics in 1930, and as his own writings attest, he had some problems (racism! paranoia!) with Mexicans and black people, who happened to be turning everyone on to reefer use in the early twentieth century in America. ("Thanks," said everyone.)

DuPont owned the largest chemical company in America. DuPont's products, from nylon to pharmaceuticals, were more expensive than products that could be made better with cannabis, and were (are) worse for the environment.

And Hearst was the owner of the largest newspaper company in the USA, and also owned huge amounts of timber acreage to make paper. Hemp, meanwhile, could produce better-quality paper in less time than timber, at less cost, and at four times the yield, all while doing way less damage to the ecosystem.

It's easy to see the common thread between these three dudes when it comes to wanting cannabis wiped out—they all had a very strong motive to do whatever it took.

So. . . .

Hearst began publishing falsified stories in his newspapers nationwide with alarming over-the-top headlines, such as, "Marijuana Goads User to Blood Lust" and "Hotel Clerk Identifies Marijuana Smoker as Gunman." He also fanned the flames on many Americans' prejudice against blacks and immigrants by spreading the untruth that marijuana-crazed blacks were routinely raping white women, and that

FROM LEFT: Harry Anslinger • William Randolf Hearst

Mexicans were all lazy and dangerous rampant pot-smokers.

DuPont's banker, Andrew Mellon, was Secretary of the Treasury under Herbert Hoover in the 1930s and was an uncle by marriage to Anslinger, who used his political influence to pass the Marijuana Tax Law of 1937, effectively banning hemp and marijuana and allowing DuPont's chemical company to supply their newly invented synthetic fiber nylon to the domestic economy without the greater competition of cannabis. The new law also succeeded in protecting Hearst's major timber and paper interests from being completely overtaken by cheaper and better hemp paper. And it paved the way for pharmaceutical companies to push dangerous, expensive (profitable) drugs on people who would benefit way more from cannabis.

These three guys succeeded in carrying out a propaganda-fueled conspiracy, ultimately increasing human destruction of the environment by producing plastic and paper and synthetic drugs that are far inferior to cannabis in terms of overall human benefit. By the 1990s, DuPont was still the largest producer of artificial fibers in the United States while no legal harvest of any textile-grade hemp has been allowed in over seventy-five years. DuPont is also a leading corporation in the pharmaceutical industry, an industry that has made billions and billions of dollars thanks to the protectionist prohibition of marijuana.

The greatest and most commonly used plant in world history—and America's traditional crop—could provide huge quantities of our textiles, paper, medicines, and hundreds more products if not for the greed of those who still want to keep it illegal today in order to stay protected from competition.

If you want to get to the bottom of any crime, just look for who has the motives.

PHARMACEUTICALS.

They don't want anyone to have easy access to cheaper, more effective, and less damaging marijuana. So they pay politicians to keep pot illegal, and can continue pushing expensive chemical-heavy prescription meds that can be good but often have terrible side effects.

SYNTHETIC FIBER.

Companies that make synthetic fibers from petroleum-based chemicals—often long on weird chemical waste and short on biodegradability—really don't want the competition of legal industrial hemp fiber being cheaply and cleanly prepared for manufacturers to make all the same products they make, only better, stronger, cheaper, and cleaner.

ALCOHOL.

Everyone—especially the alcohol industry—knows that alcohol consumption does far more damage to individuals and to society than marijuana ever could. Every accredited institution that has studied this comparison has the same results. The alcohol lobby really doesn't want to face the competition of legal marijuana for people's recreational dollars, and so they pay politicians to keep it illegal, by any means necessary.

PRISON $YSTEM.

Prisons are for-profit enterprises. That's a huge reason why America has the highest incarceration rate in the world. Land of the free? There have been hundreds of thousands of people sent to prison for marijuana alone, with about eighty percent of the convictions being for simple possession, not even dealing. The prison lobby pays elected politicians to keep marijuana illegal in order to keep feeding them inmates.

POLITICIANS.

It's irrefutable that marijuana is basically harmless to individuals, especially when used responsibly. The research papers prove it. But so many politicians are owned by the corporate lobbyists, that they refuse to do the right thing—legalize marijuana—while tens of thousands of their constituents' lives get ruined each year due to criminal records for marijuana busts. And they allow this in order to keep the rich rich, and to make a few extra bucks themselves.

Looking Up

There's always been a smart, brave minority of people who see what's really going on behind the curtain of the anti-marijuana propaganda machine, and who have spoken out against it, loudly! For decades, many good people have been doing everything they can to raise awareness about what marijuana really does and doesn't do to people.

Maybe it's the rise of the internet and the most democratic flow of information in the history of the world. Maybe all that hard work is finally paying off. And maybe it's just time.

But for the first time since before the 1930s in America, the majority of people are no longer fooled by the shady corporate lobbies of alcohol, prisons, and pharmaceutical companies. And that majority is growing.

In November 2012, citizens in two U.S. states—Washington and Colorado—voted YES to overturn the prohibition on marijuana. Legal consumption of marijuana for recreational use went into effect in Washington state on December 6, 2012, and followed in Colorado in early 2013.

Activists partied for a moment, but got right back to work in the 48 other states, many of which will have pro-marijuana bills up for vote in the next election cycle.

The people have spoken, and the chorus is getting louder and stronger.

Could it be that the nightmare of marijuana prohibition—which has destroyed millions more lives than the plant itself ever could—is nearly over?

Let go, let grow.

POTENTIAL

An empty vessel will soon be filled.

KEEPIN' IT REAL FRESH

Marijuana Storage

If you're going to invest in marijuana, and we know you will, you really should take the time to store it properly so it stays fresh and works at peak perform-ance. If stored the right way, pot can pack its usual punch a few years after it's stored—not that anyone has ever found that out.

ENVELOPE, FOLDED PAPER, ALUMINUM FOIL

The only time it's acceptable to use any of these storage methods is if not using them would cause someone to literally die. Otherwise, never use these. Ever. With one exception. If you're traveling somewhere and don't want to carry paraphernalia, it's cool to store the bud in alumi-num foil and then use the foil to build a dispos-able pipe.

PLASTIC BAGGIE

These are fine for getting your weed home from the supplier, or if you're going to smoke it all in a day or so. But if you've scored a lid that should last a week or more, you shouldn't leave it in the standard plastic baggie—the buds can get crushed, the weed dries out, and the aroma escapes. Think of it like goldfish; you don't leave them in the plastic baggie when you get them home, do you?

AIR-TIGHT JAR

Now you're talking. The air-tight glass jar is the best way to store weed on a regular basis. Get a few of them, and use the proper size depending on how much you're holding—pack them as full of bud as possible to reduce the amount of extra air. If you're using see-through jars, store them out of the light—or better than that, get dark-colored jars.

VACUUM PACK

If you have one of those food vacuum-pack machines, you can store some weed in the air-free air-tight plastic for up to a few years, and when you unseal it, it will be as real as the day you stored it. This is a good way to do secret stashes. Keep it in a cool and dark place.

LIGHT AND TEMP

Never store your buds in direct light—light kills the trichomes in the weed, and trichomes get you high.

Never store your buds above a heat source like the oven, HVAC vent, refrigerator, etc.—it dries them out.

Never store your buds in the fridge or freezer—cold destroys the trichomes, and you just learned a second ago that that is not a good thing.

LEGALIZE IT!

Cannabis Activists and Organizations

Ever since cannabis became illegal, people have been trying to get it legal again. Here are just a few of the individuals and organizations who've led the fight to do the right thing—legalize it!

INDIVIDUALS

TOM FORCADE (1945–1978)
Founder of *High Times* magazine in 1974, Tom's influence carries on decades after his passing. His magazine remains the largest and most recognizable pro-marijuana magazine in the world, and celebrated its 38th anniversary in 2012. *High Times* remains devoted to promoting both the joy and the legalization of marijuana, and its positive influence on the forward progress of marijuana cannot be understated.

AARON HOUSTON
Executive Director of Students for Sensible Drug Policy, Aaron

is a nationally recognized expert on drug policy and marijuana law, and played a key role in persuading the Department of Justice to formally issue written guidelines on medical marijuana in October 2009. Houston's work on Capitol Hill was chronicled in a 2007 Showtime documentary, *In Pot We Trust.* He was named a "Rising Star of Politics" by *Campaigns & Elections' Politics* magazine in 2008.

STEVE KUBBY
Libertarian and marijuana activist and author, Steve took his fight against cancer public in order to comprehensively show how marijuana was a large part of his management and recovery. He has authored two books on drug-policy reform—*The Politics of Consciousness* and *Why Marijuana Should Be Legal* (along with Ed Rosenthal). Kubby wrote California Proposition 215, or the Compas-

sionate Use Act of 1996, concerning the use of medical marijuana. The proposition was enacted into law on November 5, 1996.

BILL MAHER
Stand-up comedian, television host, and political commentator,

Bill is a member of the advisory boards for both NORML and the Marijuana Policy Project. He has been a longtime outspoken advocate of the legalization of marijuana, especially on his HBO television show, *Real Time with Bill Maher.*

WILLIE NELSON

Country music superstar and co-chair of the advisory board of the National Organization for the Reform of Marijuana Laws (NORML), Willie is a well-known, lifelong marijuana user and

activist. In 2005 Nelson played in a benefit golf tournament for NORML, to raise awareness about marijuana. Nelson founded the TeaPot Party for marijuana legalization in 2010 after being arrested for marijuana possession; the party's motto: "Tax It, Regulate It, and Legalize It!"

ED ROSENTHAL

Founder of Quick Trading Company—which publishes books on the cultivation, lifestyle, and legalization of marijuana (many written by Rosenthal himself, including *Why Marijuana Should Be Legal,* with Steve Kubby)—Ed is a longtime outspoken activist, horticulturist, author, and policy developer for medical marijuana. He was a columnist for *High Times* through the '80s and '90s, and has gone through several high-profile federal court cases. He twice beat federal drug convictions (on appeal) for growing medical marijuana in Oakland, California, partly because the judge withheld from jurors the fact that Rosenthal was acting in compliance with Oakland law.

STEPH SHERER

In 2002, Steph established Americans for Safe Access "with the purpose of building a strong grassroots movement to protect patients and their rights to safe and legal access" to medi-

cal marijuana. Sherer is herself a medical marijuana patient, and has lectured on the widespread legalization of medical marijuana at the University California at Berkeley and George Washington University in Washington, D.C. She was awarded the San Diego Peacemaker of the Year award in 2003.

KEITH STROUP

Attorney and founder of the National Organization for the Reform of Marijuana Laws (NORML), Stroup founded the seminal nonprofit group in 1970 using $5,000 from the Play-

boy Foundation, and served as executive director until 1979. He recently published the book, *It's NORML to Smoke Pot: The 40 Year Fight for Marijuana Smokers' Rights,* which details the history of NORML's forty-year fight for legal marijuana policy.

Dr. Tod Mikuriya in 2003, a supporter of medical marijuana (Note: he died in 2007)

AMERICAN MEDICAL MARIJUANA ASSOCIATION

Established in 1999 in Fort Bragg, California, by Steve Kubby, Ed Rosenthal, and Tod H. Mikuriya, AMMA is at the forefront of the battle to protect the rights of medical cannabis patients. The volunteer group recently received official recognition by the United States government as one of the top organizational websites promoting medical marijuana law reform.

AMERICANS FOR SAFE ACCESS

Established in 2002 in Oakland, California, by Steph Sherer, ASA is a grassroots movement that works to protect patients' rights to safe and legal access to medical marijuana. ASA is the largest national member-based organization of patients, medical professionals, scientists, and concerned citizens promoting safe and legal access to cannabis for therapeutic use and research, with the immediate goal of helping patients and their providers, and the long-term goal of comprehensive medical marijuana legality.

HIGH TIMES MAGAZINE

Established in 1974 in New York City, New York, by Tom Forcade, *High Times* was originally meant as a joke, but soon found a broad audience. Published monthly, the magazine is devoted to the pleasures of marijuana, as well as promoting legalization. It is the largest marijuana-themed magazine in the world, and sponsors many popular marijuana-related events, including The High Times Cannabis Cup, The High Times Medical Cannabis Cup, The High Times Stony Awards, The High Times World Stoner Games, and The High Times Doobie Awards, just to name a few.

MARIJUANA POLICY PROJECT (MPP)

Established in 1995 in Washington, D.C., by Rob Kampia, Chuck Thomas, and Mike Kirshner, MPP is now the largest marijuana policy reform organization in the United States, based on the size of its budget, membership, and staff. MPP's goal is to work through the political system in order to make marijuana a legally regulated entity, similar to alcohol, and to ensure individuals who use it for medical purposes can obtain and use it safely without fear of arrest. It has spearheaded ballot initiatives and lobbying efforts in states across the country, and it has been responsible for changing most state-level marijuana laws since 2000.

NATIONAL ORGANIZATION FOR THE REFORM OF MARIJUANA LAWS (NORML)

Established in 1970 in Washington, D.C., by Keith Stroup, and funded by $5,000 from the Playboy Foundation. NORML's main goal is to educate the public in order to achieve a political consensus to legalize recreational use of marijuana in the United States so that the responsible use of cannabis by adults is no longer subject to legal penalty and social stigma. NORML is one of the largest and most famous activist groups in the USA, with a grassroots network of 135 chapters and over 550 lawyers.

ssdp

STUDENTS FOR SENSIBLE DRUG POLICY

Established in 1998 in Washington, D.C., by a small group of students at the Rochester Institute of Technology and George Washington University, SSDP is now an international non-profit advocacy and education organization with offices in Washington D.C. and Mexico City. SSDP has chapter networks in universities, colleges, and high schools around the world that organize student and teacher activism to promote sensible change in attitudes toward marijuana policy and education, with a focus on fighting the government's counterproductive "War on Drugs."

Let's Get Political
RESPONSIBILITY IS A HEAVY RESPONSIBILITY

In American democracy, when something ain't right the people have the right to tell the man it's wrong. So put the pen to paper, or fingertips to computer keys, or finger-swipes to smart screens, and send a letter or email to your state and federal representatives the next time a bill comes up for vote.

To the Honorable [YOUR REPRESENTATIVE'S NAME]:

Hello,

My name is [YOUR NAME], and I live in [STATE + DISTRICT]. I am writing to ask that you support [NUMBER AND NAME OF BILL].

I feel that people who use marijuana are unfairly criminalized, and the "War on Drugs" is a complete failure.

For over seventy years, our country's marijuana laws have not curtailed marijuana use, but they have put many good and decent people in prison. As you surely know, in the 1930s the original (yet mostly secretive) reasons to make marijuana illegal were racism against minorities and protecting corporate wealth—and unfortunately, both factors still exist, though the difference today is that the light of truth is shown upon these nefarious reasons. Still, today, almost a million people are arrested for marijuana each year, and almost ninety percent of those arrests are for mere possession, not manufacture or sale.

Even after the federal government has spent hundreds of billions of dollars on the War on Drugs, the marijuana usage rate in the U.S. is the highest in the world. And, according to all scientific evidence, marijuana is far safer than both alcohol and cigarettes, and therefore should be subject to similar laws and regulations.

I urge you to cosponsor and vote for [NAME OF LEGISLATION] in order to put an end to marijuana prohibition. I will greatly appreciate your support on this issue, and will be watching to see how you vote.

Thank you,
[YOUR NAME]
[YOUR ADDRESS]

TURN TO PAGE 155

LOOK WHO'S TOKIN'

Sweet Smell of Success

With so many people smoking weed regularly for the last few centuries, odds are that a few of them might rise up and actually accomplish something—despite the propaganda that says weed leads to failure, insanity, murder, and mayhem. Yeah, right. Turns out, there are tons of achievers who love their cheeba, whether they do it daily or only occasionally. Without stoners the world would be a far less interesting place. And with weed comes all kinds of great art, thought, science, and more.

LOUIS ARMSTRONG
One of the greatest jazz musicians of all time smoked weed daily for most of his life, including before performances and recordings.

THE BEATLES
Before Bob Dylan turned the Beatles on to pot, they were writing pretty little ditties like "Love Me Do" and "I Wanna Hold Your Hand." After meeting Mary Jane, they started getting into the really good stoner stuff like "Lucy in the Sky with Diamonds" and "Magical Mystery Tour" and "Across the Universe." Thanks, Bob.

MICHAEL BLOOMBERG
Asked if he smoked pot when he was a young man, the longtime mayor of New York City replied, "You bet I did. And I enjoyed it."

SIR RICHARD BRANSON
The billionaire British entertainment and travel mogul is an occasional pot smoker and an outspoken supporter of legalization. Talk about hip; he learned how to roll a joint from Keith Richards of the Rolling Stones.

FRANCIS CRICK
The Nobel Prize winner for discovering the double-helix structure of DNA, Crick used both marijuana and LSD to remove the filters of abstract thought. He also was a founding member of the cannabis-legalization group, Soma.

SALVADORE DALI
The trailblazing Spanish painter was reportedly a blazer. Or was

he more than that? After all, he did say, "I don't do drugs. I am drugs." And he liked to paint melting clocks and other visionary things.

RODNEY DANGERFIELD
One of the most popular comedians in U.S. history smoked pot for 62 years, claiming that it helped with anxiety. But don't blame his nervous onstage demeanor on pot; he never smoked before performing.

ALEXANDRE DUMAS
French author of *The Three Musketeers* was a big cannabis fan, and used it for inspiration in writing his classic novels. He also encouraged others to use it, and was a member of the Hash Club, or "Le Club des Haschishins."

RICHARD FEYNMAN
Besides being one of the physicists who developed the atomic bomb, Feynman used marijuana

to enhance his out-of-body experiences in a sensory-deprivation tank, and his resulting theory of quantum electrodynamics earned him a Nobel Prize.

JANE FONDA
The iconoclastic actress and activist has always been someone who smokes pot whenever she wants to and doesn't care what anyone thinks or says about it. Same goes for her brother, Peter Fonda—but you already knew that.

FRANCIS FORD COPPOLA
One of the greatest filmmakers of all time said he turned to marijuana for physical and mental relief during the famously insane production of the film *Apocalypse Now*. Coincidentally, many film watchers turn to marijuana before watching *Apocalypse Now*.

MORGAN FREEMAN
One of the most bankable actors in the world used to have a hard-drug problem, but he beat it. He'll "never give up the ganja,"

though, he told *The Guardian*, calling it "God's own weed."

BILL GATES
The founder of Microsoft—whose influence touches everyone on the planet—has never directly, publicly confirmed that he smokes or smoked weed. But he did hint very strongly that he used marijuana, during an interview with *Playboy* magazine. Not that anyone read the interview.

STEPHEN JAY GOULD
The great paleontologist, biologist, and historian started using pot after being diagnosed with cancer, and proceeded to use it for the next twenty years, stating that it had an "important effect" on his recovery, and even becoming a vocal advocate for legalizing medical marijuana. By the way, he was using pot regularly when he wrote the incredibly smart book, *The Structure of Evolutionary Theory*.

STEVE JOBS
The founder of Apple Computers and one of the most influential Americans of the last century was a well-known marijuana fanboy, at least in his early days. Hell, he even dated Joan Baez.

JOHN F. KENNEDY
Easily the hippest-ever president of the United States (besides Barack Obama), they say JFK had a thing for THC.

STEPHEN KING
Pot critics say that weed universally destroys motivation and makes you lazy. So how do you explain how reported pot fan Stephen King could write tens of thousands of pages of fiction in over fifty novels and short stories, and sell nearly half a billion copies of his work? Note: Though he did tell *High Times* in 2003 that he didn't use ot anymore.

LADY GAGA
The top pop star in recent memory, Gaga is a proud fiend who credits weed as her muse when writing music, smokes up on stage in front of huge audiences, and in October 2012 she tweeted, "So I was weed for Halloween . . . Princess High the Cannabis Queen."

VICTOR HUGO
One of the greatest novelists of all time, the French author of *Les Misérables* was a frequent smoker and a member of the famous Le Club des Haschishins, the Hash Club.

KENNEDY CENTER HONORS, 2008

The Kennedy Center Honors is not a person; it's an annual awards event hosted by the president of the United States where a few big-time entertainers receive a lifetime achievement award. But the 2008 edition is one for the pot ages, with a bunch of staunch stoners. Its honorees featured Barbra Streisand, Pete Townshend, Morgan Freeman, and George Jones—all of whom were keen pot smokers at some point during their careers. The VIP performers that night included Rob Thomas, Joss Stone, and Jack Black—all major stoners today. And the presiding president was George W. Bush, who inhaled a lot of weed in his pre-politics career as a frat-boy-man.

BRUCE LEE

The world's greatest martial artist liked weed and kicked ass.

MODIGLIANI

The famous Italian painter, whose works appear in great museums around the world, was a total iconoclast and regular cannabis smoker, among other things.

BARACK OBAMA

Yes, he smoked pot. And yes, he inhaled. Frequently. "That was the point," he said.

MICHAEL PHELPS

This stoner swimmer is only the most decorated medalist in the history of the Olympic Games.

PABLO PICASSO

One of the world's greatest artists is said to have conceived of cubism—a new form that changed the direction of art—while high on hashish. And it's known that he painted the famous work *Family of Saltimbanques* high on cannabis.

DIEGO RIVERA

The great Mexican artist was a regular user of marijuana. In Erroll Flynn's autobiography, he writes of the night Rivera turned him on to a marijuana joint before showing the actor his paintings, and said, "After smoking this you will see a painting and you will hear it as well."

OLIVER SACKS

Sacks is a multi-decorated scientist, professor, and bestselling author. His memoir *Awakenings* was made into a popular film of the same title, with Robin Williams and Robert De Niro. He's on record saying that he used marijuana on a recreational level and beyond, and sees it as a possible means to understanding deeper consciousness.

CARL SAGAN

The famous scientist and best-selling author—winner of the Pullitzer Prize, and an Emmy for the TV show *Cosmos*—was also a famously outspoken stoner who had many great insights under the influence of cannabis.

PETER SELLERS

One of the greatest actors of the twentieth century was a regular stoner. He learned to stop worrying and love the bong.

WILLIAM SHAKESPEARE

"Is this a doobie which I see before me?"

Facts are mounting that show Shakespeare—one of the greatest and most prolific writers of all time—was a pot smoker. Exhibit A: Archaeologists have found clay pipes with cannabis resin in Shakespeare's garden in Stratford-upon-Avon, dating to the time that he lived there. Exhibit B: *A Midsummer Night's Dream*.

KEVIN SMITH

The influential filmmaker came to cannabis relatively later in life. Never a smoker in his teens and twenties, in his book *Tough Shit* he talks about his newfound love of regular weed consumption, with the caveat that he can get high as long as he's doing something, and not just vegging out. (Wait a minute; isn't "vegging out" doing something?)

RICK STEVES

America's most widely read travel writer is also a proud pot smoker and activist. Early in his career, he stumped for marijuana decriminalization incognito. But at some point, he said "fuck it" and became a vocal, visible activist—and even became a board member of NORML.

JUSTIN TIMBERLAKE

The childhood Mouseketeer, teen singing sensation, and adult A-list actor and pop star, has also been an avid pot star. He admittedly was sky high during the hidden-camera taping of the TV show *Punk'd*, when he was the target of a fake FBI takeover of his mansion. It's must-see TV. He quit smoking weed after that, but resumed later, saying "Sometimes I have a brain that needs to be turned off."

TED TURNER

Founder of CNN, owner of the Atlanta Braves, and holder of many other big accomplishments

as an earthling, Turner has been an unapologetic pot smoker and is a major donor to the Kentucky Hemp Museum.

JOHN UPDIKE

The author of dozens of novels—and winner of multiple Pulitzer Prizes and National Book Awards—typed and toked, according to his memoir, *Self-Consciousness*.

QUEEN VICTORIA

The namesake of an era of cool furniture and clothes and other stuff, Victoria's physician prescribed cannabis for her menstrual cramps and other various ailments. She loved it.

DR. ANDREW WEIL

The popular white-bearded naturopath, medicinal herbs expert, and

bestselling author often appears on TV and once wrote for *High Times* magazine. With medical degrees from Harvard, the proud pot smoker has spoken out about the advantages of marijuana for creative thought and positive altered consciousness.

MONTEL WILLIAMS

The popular TV host didn't start smoking grass until his forties. He was diagnosed with MS in 1999 and got sick from all the chemical medication. Pot was the only thing that helped that had no side effects. He's now one of the most vocal activists for legalization, and still a pretty smooth dude.

GEORGE WASHINGTON

The first president of the United States absolutely grew cannabis on his Virginia plantation. But whether or not he got high may not be one-hundred percent provable, although we think he did, thanks to a couple of confirmed quotations. "The artificial preparation of hemp, from Silesia [present-day Poland], is really a curiosity," Washington said, most likely talking about hashish and getting high. Would he have called cotton or trees a "curiosity"? He also wrote in his journal that he "began to separate the male from the female plants," because, of course, the females are the ones that have THC and get you high.

DOODLE TIME

Take a toke, pick a pen, and doodle down. The theme for this page is . . .

Cannabis Leaves

EVERY HOUR, IT'S 4:20 SOMEWHERE

The Legend of 420

Every day, lots of people get together with friends to smoke weed at 4:20 p.m. And every year there are parties and festivals around the world on 4/20 (April 20) where stoners celebrate their shared love of marijuana.

The number gets referenced all over pop culture—like in the movie *Pulp Fiction*, where every clock visible in the movie is set to 4:20; and on the TV show *The Price Is Right*, where a number of stoner contestants over the years have repeatedly (and hilariously) guessed the price $420 for every item up for bid.

The term 420 is used by stoners in lots of ways. To make connections in mixed company, "Are you 420-friendly?" To tell friends it's time to get high, "Hey, it's 420 time!" To ask if someone has any pot on them, "Got any 420?"

But exactly why is the magic number 420 celebrated by stoners here, there, and everywhere? What does it mean, and where does it come from?

People used to say that 420 was California state police code for a marijuana bust. The fact is, that was a myth and has zero truth behind it. The real story has been around here and there, and was told in detail in the last few years.

The 420 Story

The legend dates back to 1971, when a small group of friends who were students at San Rafael High School in California—each of them one part athlete, one part stoner—began to meet every afternoon after they finished practice for their various sports. They would meet near a wall outside school, and started calling themselves the "Waldos" in honor of the wall. The friends' purpose each afternoon was to head out into the Point Reyes forest to find a hidden crop of marijuana plants that was supposedly abandoned by its owner. And to get stoned.

In the beginning, they gave each other reminders throughout the day about the meeting time—4:20 p.m. Soon they started using the number "420" ("four-twenty") to stand for the act of smoking weed at any time of day, and then the number became a synonym for weed itself.

So how did the term spread from a circle of five high school students in San Rafael, California, to the entire planet's circle of stoners?

Deadheads, of course.

As it turns out, two of the five friends had a direct connection to the Grateful Dead. Mark Gravitch's father handled real estate for some of the Dead. And Dave Reddix's brother Patrick was musical friends with Dead bassist Phil Lesh. Because of these connections, the Waldos were invited to many Dead parties, rehearsals, and other insider gatherings. They naturally used the 420 term among themselves when passing joints around, and it must have caught on among the Dead and their friends and roadies, and from there, it spread to Deadheads across the planet.

Eventually *High Times* magazine got wind of the term, and started planning events based on 4/20 each year, like the World Hemp Expo Extravaganza and the Cannabis Cup. In the early '90s, *High Times* secured the web domain 420.com, and the magazine's overall reach and influence made the term—and the date, and the time—an international connecting point for all stoners.

By 1998, the original Waldos had become very aware that their personal little code word had become a worldwide cannabis-culture phenomenon, and decided to tell the whole story. They contacted *High Times* magazine, and then-editor Steve Hager flew to San Rafael to meet the group. After seeing the evidence—including a handmade flag with "420" on it and letters postmarked in 1971 filled with 420 references—Hager was convinced.

Today, the original 420 friends—also including Steve Capper and Patty Young—are famous and proud of their impact on cannabis culture, although none of them smokes grass like they used to.

No matter, there are millions of people who gladly take the mantle for them—every day at 4:20 p.m., and every April 20.

Celebrating 420

Many stoners do something special every April 20 to toast the feast day of marijuana. It's a day to celebrate nature, community, creativity, and peace, and also to get a little political. If you're on board but don't know all the options available to make the most of the day, here are a few things to try:

GATHERINGS

Festivals, rallies, concerts, smokeouts, stoner-movie screenings, themed comedy shows, and more are scheduled all over the world. Bigger cities will have the big gatherings, but lots of small-town stoners celebrate the day together, too. A little online research should yield a good crop of activities to choose from.

D.I.Y.

If you can't find an established event nearby, or just can't get to one, gather some friends and do it yourself. Rent some stoner videos and have a movie marijuanathon. Go to a park, a lake, or anywhere in nature for a pot picnic. Or just throw a 420-themed party with cannabis-leaf party favors, classic stoner snacks, and other creative twists.

GET POLITICAL

While 4/20 is totally a time to celebrate, it's also a good day to focus on the fight to get it legal. You can take some time on 4/20 to join a national marijuana activist group, like NORML, and/or send donations to several groups. Use the day as a reminder to sit down and write letters to your state and national representatives in government, including the POTUS. And if you're really up for it, set up a political pot party, invite some friends over, and help them write their own letters to the government—supply a sample letter, and go online to help everyone find contact info for their reps.

FLYING SOLO

If you find yourself alone on the 4/20 holiday, just spark up at twenty minutes after any hour—you'll know there is an entire time zone of stoners somewhere celebrating with you at that moment.

POT BUSTS
of the
RICH and FAMOUS

As ineffective as it really is, the War on Drugs has still managed to mess up millions of people's lives by putting an arrest on their record—or worse—just for smoking or possessing a little weed. And Johnny Law especially loves to stick a feather in his cap when big-name busts get covered in the news, like these newsmakers below, most of whom don't have any business being called criminals for these "crimes."

KAREEM ABDUL-JABBAR. One of the best basketball players in NBA history, and a longtime migraine sufferer, Kareem was busted for marijuana possession in Canada (1998) and the U.S. (2000), and got misdemeanor charges.

LOUIS ARMSTRONG. The jazz legend was arrested in 1931 for marijuana possession, which totally blows. But ultimately the charge was suspended.

HOYT AXTON. The country musician/actor and his wife were arrested in 1997 at their Montana house with just over a pound of marijuana, which he used to help ease stress and pain following a 1995 stroke. They were fined and their sentences were deferred.

DAVID BOWIE. The Thin White Duke was arrested in 1976 with about a half-pound of grass on

him. He was facing a maximum of fifteen years in the slammer, but the charges were dropped. Wham bam thank you, ma'am.

JAMES BROWN. The hardest working man in show business needed to relax at some point. And while relaxing with "just a

little tiny bit" of herb in 1998, he was arrested on charges of marijuana possession. He told reporters that he used marijuana for medicinal purposes to help ease the pain from bad eyes, and later, the charges were dropped and he got back to work.

LENNY BRUCE. The blue comic got arrested for possessing the green in 1961 and '63, and was hounded by the cops for most of his adult life for all kinds of charges, many of them trumped up. He died at age 39, according to Phil Spector, of "an overdose of police."

NEIL CASSADY. The Beat author offered a few joints to an undercover cop in a San Fran nightclub and ended up in San Quentin prison for two years. Just a stupid waste of taxpayer resources—wasting a cop's entire day on the stakeout when he could have been fighting actual crimes, and then blowing thousands of dollars to keep the poor guy locked up—to stop a guy from trying to make someone happy.

TOMMY CHONG. In 2003, Tommy Chong was the victim of one of the most brutal judicial decisions in the history of drug arrests—because the conviction didn't even involve drugs! Chong's successful online glass pipe business, Nice Dreams, was the target—along with around fifty similar businesses nationwide—of what the U.S. Attorneys' office called "Operation Pipe Dreams." Cute name, guys. For selling 7,500 glass bongs and pipes, Chong was fined $20,000, had to forfeit over $100,000 in cash and all of his wares, and spent nine months in prison. All

for selling pipes which, technically speaking—which is all that usually matters in jurisprudence—could have been used for tobacco.

TONY CURTIS. The actor most famous for dressing in drag in *Some Like It Hot*, with Marilyn Monroe, got busted with bud in Britain in 1970. He should have had a secret compartment built into his purse.

MITCH DANIEL. The current governor of Indiana smoked pot while he was a student at Princeton, and got busted for possession in 1970, spending a couple of nights in jail for his troubles.

BOB DENVER. Gilligan from the TV show *Gilligan's Island* got busted in 1998 after he signed for a delivery package containing marijuana. The funny thing is, the sender was Dawn Wells—a.k.a. Mary Ann from the show—but Denver never gave her up in court. Luckily for all, he only got six months' probation. Mr. Howell was ready to bail him out if needed.

NEIL DIAMOND. The singer with amazing hair was busted in a 1976 raid on his house, which produced under an ounce of marijuana. Nice job wasting taxpayer dollars there, boys. The arrest was struck from his record after he attended a six-month drug program—another waste of taxpayer money!

SNOOP DOGG. It was only a matter of time—each of several times—before Snoop got busted for possession of marijuana. But

two of the cases stand out. In January 2012, he was busted at the same Texas border stop where Willie Nelson was busted, just a few years after the two

musicians collaborated on the song and video "My Medicine." And in June of that year, he got nabbed in Norway for possession, and received a two-year ban from that country. Which begs the question: What the hell was Snoop Dogg doing in Norway?

DONOVAN. They called him "Mellow Yellow" for a reason. In 1966, the Scottish folkie won the honor of being the first big British pop star to get busted for marijuana possession, and was banned from the U.S. for almost two years because of the stigma.

FREDDY FENDER. In yet another horribly unbalanced conviction for marijuana possession, the popular musician with one of the sweetest hairdos in music history was busted in 1960 with two freaking joints and ended up spending almost three freaking years at the Angola prison farm in Louisiana. Governor Jimmie Davis, also a songwriter, later pardoned Fender and he was released.

THE GRATEFUL DEAD. The entire band got busted for possessing "sugar magnolia" a few times. The first came in 1967 when the house they all shared in San Francisco was raided on a tip. Some members of the band, but not Jerry Garcia, were arrested, and the charges were soon dropped. They were arrested again in their hotel room in Hawaii after a performance; again, Garcia managed to escape the charge. None of the guys did any time for their "crime."

ART GARFUNKEL. This cat from the musical duo Simon and Garfunkel, and best known for his amazing white-guy afro, was arrested for marijuana possession in 2004 and again in 2005.

WOODY HARRELSON. The proud pot smoker was arrested in 1996 for planting four cannabis hemp seeds in Kentucky. His goal was to teach the government a lesson in botany, by challenging a law that didn't distinguish between marijuana and the mostly THC-free hemp. The charge was dismissed, but the government didn't learn anything.

GEORGE HARRISON. The Beatle and his wife Patty Boyd were arrested in 1969 at their home in London for marijuana possession. According to Harrison, the 120 joints that were "found" were actually planted by the police, and that they never found his actual stash that was on premises. The overzealous cop—Sergeant Pilcher—who was also responsible for John Lennon's arrest the year before, was later arrested himself and convicted of planting drugs on many victims of his bogus arrests.

ALLEN IVERSON. A good friend of Basketball Jones, the little NBA star with the big heart and bigger lungs got caught with a big bag of pot in 1997. He did a bunch of hours of community service to get off.

MICK JAGGER. The Rolling Stones front man was arrested in 1967 and 1970 for marijuana possession, but got off both times after spending just one night in jail for the first bust.

KEN KESEY. The leader of the Merry Pranksters, and author of such classic books as *One Flew Over the Cukoo's Nest*, Kesey was arrested in 1965 for marijuana possession in California. But he pulled another prank, faking his suicide for the cops' benefit by having his friends leave his truck parked near a cliff with a suicide note inside; meanwhile, he fled to Mexico. Upon returning eight months later, he was arrested, convicted, and spent five months in a county jail before hiring a well-known marijuana attorney and getting released.

TIMOTHY LEARY. The psychologist and champion of LSD (he studied it at Harvard before it became illegal) was first arrested for marijuana possession in 1965 when he took the rap for his daughter, who was holding a very small amount in her underwear as they tried to enter the U.S. from Mexico. He was sentenced to thirty years in prison—thirty years!—given a $30,000 fine, and ordered to undergo psychiatric treatment. He appealed the case and the sentence was later overturned. In 1968, he was arrested again, this time in Laguna Beach, California, for possession of two marijuana roaches—two roaches!—which he claims were planted on him by the arresting officer. He was later sentenced for the two-roach bust to ten years in prison, with

another ten years added for a prior arrest, and ordered to serve the twenty years consecutively. Twenty years! For two roaches! He escaped from a low-security prison in 1970 and went on the run to several countries outside the U.S. He was captured by U.S. officials in Afghanistan in 1973 and deported back to the States, where he was held on $5 million bail thanks to President Nixon calling him "the most dangerous man in America." (Look who's talking.) He was sent to Folsom Prison in California and faced a 95-year sentence, but Governor Jerry Brown ordered his release in 1976.

JOHN LENNON. The Beatle was arrested along with wife Yoko Ono in 1968 for possession of 200 grams of hash in their London flat. Lennon plead guilty and paid a one-hundred-fifty pound fine. In 1972, paranoid U.S. President Richard Nixon set in motion plans to deport Lennon from the U.S., citing the 1968 misdemeanor conviction in London as the reason, and on March 23, 1973, the U.S. government ordered Lennon

to leave the country within sixty days. Nixon's crimes involving the Watergate scandal soon were uncovered, though, and led to his impeachment. The next president, Gerald Ford, had no interest in continuing the deportation plan, and in 1975 Lennon was granted the right to remain in the one place in the world he wanted to be—New York City.

BOB MARLEY. Surprisingly, the most famous pot-smoking musician of all time only got arrested for possession once, in London in 1977. Coincidentally, during his two-year stay in England in the mid-seventies, he recorded two awesome stoner albums, *Exodus* and *Kaya*.

PAUL MCCARTNEY. The Beatle was busted with marijuana a few times, but none was as bad as the bust in Japan in 1980 almost was, when he was caught with nearly eight ounces of weed in his luggage. If tried and convicted in Japan, he likely would have faced up to seven years in prison there. But he was deported and told never to return to that country (although he did return, and performed there, a decade later).

MATTHEW MCCONAUGHEY. The *Dazed and Confused* actor had the cops called on him one night in 1999, at 2:30 a.m., for excessive noise. Turns out, he was playing the bongos naked. And when he resisted arrest for that infraction,

the cops searched his house and arrested him for marijuana possession. He beat the pot charge, but had to pay $50 for the loud bongo playing. Kind of ironic that he beat the bong charge but could not beat the bongo.

ROBERT MITCHUM. One of the greatest actors in Hollywood history was also the victim of one of the most famous busts—and most ridiculous sentences—in marijuana history. By September of 1948, Mitchum had become a Hollywood superstar. While relaxing with actress Lila Leeds and some kind buds, the duo were caught in a sting operation by the police, and Mitchum was convicted and

sentenced to prison. He spent a week in county jail, and then forty-three days on a California prison farm, before the Los Angeles District Attorney's office exposed his arrest as a set-up and overturned the conviction.

BILL MURRAY. In 1970, while a student at Regis University in Colorado, he was arrested at Chicago's O'Hare Airport for trying to smuggle nearly nine pounds of marijuana. If anyone who ever lived on planet Earth could ever talk their way out of getting caught smuggling nine pounds of marijuana, it's Bill Murray. And he did. He got off with a misdemeanor and five years' probation.

WILLIE NELSON. The world-famous country singer—and current co-chair of the NORML advisory board—was busted at the Texas border in 2006 for possession of 1.5 pounds of marijuana and several ounces of mushrooms, fined just over a thousand bucks, and placed on probation for six months. But it could have been much worse, if not for the quick thinking of his band and crew, who all claimed ownership of the drugs. The amounts confiscated were enough for a felony if possessed by one person, but since five others claimed possession, Nelson's charges dropped to a misdemeanor.

PAUL REUBENS. Best known to America as the character Pee-Wee Herman—and best known to stoners as the snooty desk clerk in *Cheech and Chong's Next Movie* and Howie Hamburger Dude in *Cheech and Chong's Nice Dreams*—Reubens was arrested in 1983 for marijuana possession, and got probation. This bust had nothing to do with Pee-Wee's

more infamous arrest for indulging in self-abuse in a Florida adult movie theater in 1991. As stupid as it is to arrest someone for having marijuana, even we have to admit that it's stupider to arrest someone for jerking off in an adult movie theater.

KEITH RICHARDS. Despite all of his hard-drug use and troubles with the law, the Rolling Stones' guitarist was only sent to prison once, and that was for marijuana. Keef and friends, including Mick Jagger, were raided at Keef's Sussex estate. In June 1967, Keef was sentenced to one year in prison for allowing marijuana to be smoked on his property, and was taken directly to Wormwood Scrubs Prison in London. He made bail the next day, and his conviction was overturned on appeal.

DAVID LEE ROTH. The acrobatic Van Halen front man was arrested in 1993 after buying some weed from an undercover cop in New York City's Washington Square Park. Isn't that the roadies' job? Diamond Dave's description of the purchase was, "Ten dollars' worth of Jamaican bunk reefer, man."

CARLOS SANTANA. The guitar god was busted in 1991 at the Houston Airport for carrying five grams of marijuana from Mexico. Five grams? That's not

even enough to roll one quarter-pounder doobie!

DIONNE WARWICK. In 2002, the legendary singer was detained at the Miami International Airport when about a dozen joints were found in her bag. The charges were dropped after she agreed to do public service announcements warning against illegal drug use. If you look closely at the PSAs, you can see she has her fingers crossed.

DAWN WELLS. Mary Ann from *Gilligan's Island* was not just an alleged "dealer" (see the Bob Denver bust on page 51), but she was also an alleged toker. The brunette castaway was arrested in 2007 during a traffic stop, and four joints and a few containers of marijuana were uncovered in her car. She went to jail after failing a field sobriety test, was fined $410.50 (couldn't they have just made it an even $420?), and placed on probation for six months. "Oh, my," said Mrs. Howell.

Up in Smoke

by Cheech & Chong

INTRO
A7 add6   D add4

    D   G   D

Up in smoke - that's where my money goes

      D   A7 add 6

In my lungs and sometimes up my nose

      D   D7   G

When troubled times begin to bother me

      D   A7   D add4

I take a toke and all my cares go up in smoke

E add4
      E   A   E

Up in smoke - donde todos es mi rey

        E   B7 add4

There are no signs que dice no fumer

      E   E7   A

So I roll un "bomber" - y me doy, un buen toke-ay

      E   B7   E

Y despues I choke y todos mis cares go up in smoke -

    add4

come on let's go get high!

Up in smoke - that's where I wanna be

Cause when I'm high the world below don't
   bother me

When life begins to be one long and
   dangerous road

I take a toke and all my cares go up in smoke

add4   add 4 E   B7   E

  I take a toke and all my cares go up in smoke...

Connect-the-Pot-Seeds

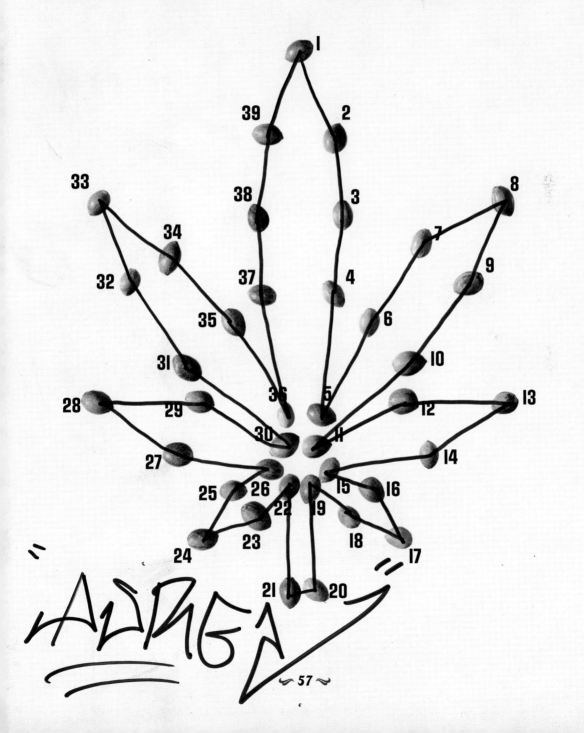

WHERE IS IT LEGAL?

ARGENTINA Small amounts legal for personal use.

BELGIUM Decriminalized for adults.

CANADA Legal for medical use.

CHILE Legal for medical use and private consumption.

COLOMBIA Decriminalized for personal comsumption.

CZECH REPUBLIC Decriminalized and medically acceptable.

ECUADOR Possession is not illegal.

INDIA Illegal but widely used in holy festivals.

ISRAEL Medical use allowed.

MEXICO Personal use of up to five grams is legal.

NEPAL Illegal but widely used.

THE NETHERLANDS Cannabis is sold in "coffee shops" but possession is illegal.

PERU Up to eight grams is legal.

SWITZERLAND The cantons Vaud, Neuchatel, Geneva, and Fribourg allow the growing and cultivation of up to 4 cannabis plants per person.

URUGUAY Possession for personal use is not penalized.

AUSTRALIA Decriminalized for personal use in Australian Capital Territory, South Australia, Western Australia, Western Australia, and the Northern Territory.

PLACES WITH THE STIFFEST PENALTIES

CHINA

Roughly 500 people are estimated to be executed for drug related offences each year.

INDONESIA

A possible 4 to 12 years in prison for possession of less than one kilogram. Anything more warrants life in prison.

IRAN

The punishment for a few grams is seventy lashes.

JAPAN

1 joint is punished by 5 years in jail. Foreigners are deported.

MALAYSIA

With seventeen ounces of marijuana or more, an individual could be punished with an execution by hanging.

PHILIPPINES

Those caught with 17 ounces or more of marijuana or .3 ounces of marijuana resin are sentenced to anything from 12 years to death.

SAUDI ARABIA

Drug possession earns a public flogging and drug dealing can warrant a public beheading. Foreigners are deported

THAILAND

Though the punishment for possession isn't as serious as in the other countries listed, Thai police have the power (and regularly use it) to search anyone they deem suspicious for marijuana, including a urine test. If caught, they have the right to issue thousand dollar fines.

VIETNAM

Being found with marijuana, an individual will be sent to "rehabilitation" which includes forced labor and starvation.

How Marijuana Works

WHY DO YOU GET HIGH?

$$HO \quad\quad (CH_2)_4CH_3$$

$$H_3C$$

$$H$$

$$O$$

$$H$$

$$H_3C \quad CH_3$$

Every stoner will tell you there's nothing like the feeling of being high. But most stoners can't tell you exactly how smoking or eating or vaporizing the buds of the cannabis plant get you high.

Whether or not someone is aware of all the chemical reactions that take you from plain reality to blissfully wacky, it still works. But it's worth it to take a minute to understand the basic science of marijuana.

Marijuana is the preparation of the *Cannabis sativa* plant intended for use as a psychoactive drug for recreational and medicinal purposes. The active ingredient in marijuana is the naturally occurring chemical "tetrahydrocannabinol," commonly known as THC.

THC is considered a "cannabinoid," which is part of a class of compounds that activate cannabinoid receptors in the human body to create changes in the brain and other organs. Cannabinoids are produced naturally in the body, synthetically by scientists, and most commonly, naturally in nature in the form of THC in cannabis.

THC causes moderate pain-relieving effects; produces feelings of relaxation via the central nervous system; stimulates the appetite; reduces aggression; and alters the senses of sight, sound, and smell. And despite the fact that this chemical compound can cause such big changes to the body, there has never been a documented fatality from consumption of marijuana via THC in its natural form. On the other hand, there have been several deaths attributed to the synthetic cannabinoid Marinol, produced by pharmaceutical companies for profit, when free cannabis would do a better job for free. Go figure.

Now, this is the part of the page where the technical scientific description of "getting high" should go. But really, using all the proper scientific terms—like "secondary metabolites" and "partial agonistic activity" and "inhibition of adenylate cyclase"—would just confuse us and confuse you and cause a major buzzkill to anyone who got this far on this page.

So, to put it simply, when you smoke or vaporize cannabis in a joint or bowl or bong or vaporizer, within a couple seconds the THC goes into your lungs then into your heart then into your bloodstream then into your brain where the THC activates the chemical cannabinoid receptors and causes feelings of euphoria, giddiness, loss of inhibition, increased relaxation, decreased stress and anxiety, enhanced appetite, and more good stuff.

And when you eat cannabis—after cooking it—it takes a bit longer for the THC to get to your brain since it first has to pass through the digestive system. Some weed-eaters feel the effects within about twenty minutes; others start feeling the effects after up to an hour. Many say the buzz from eating weed is different than smoking it, causing a more full-body sensation and more psychoactive experiences.

At the end of the day, this is all what the scientists say, and we appreciate that. But if you ask us how marijuana works . . . it's magic.

A MILLION THINGS

Anyone will tell you that all kinds of things happen when you're doing the reefer, and the cool thing is, the stuff everyone's into doing is all over the map. Now we can't say we've done it all, at least not yet, so we're putting together this bucket list. And if you can think of something to do that we forgot to include, let us know and we'll do it together.

Finger puppets

Doodle

Stare at your face in the mirror

Make a snack

Pack another bowl

Watch TV

Have sex

Play with a yoyo

Call a friend and talk about random shit

Make a sculpture

Stare at the night sky till you see a shooting star

Check the refrigerator

Play video games

Walk through an art museum

Play bongos on paint cans

Go to an amusement park

Talk to your plants

Go to an empty playground to swing, slide, and climb

Watch a scary movie

Go hiking

Take a sauna

Give a massage

Jump on a trampoline

Close your eyes and spin around until you get dizzy

Stare at the night sky and make up new constellations

Roll another one

Walk through the grass barefoot

Drink fresh-squeezed juice

Just lay there

Watch *The Three Stooges*

See a band

Draw your pet

Watch a stoner movie

Look for faces in clouds

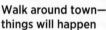

Walk around town—things will happen

Go to a Dead cover-band show

Draw a maze

Practice rolling joints

Do some tai chi

Walk the dog

Skinny dip in the ocean at night

Visit the zoo

Procrastinate

Do some gardening

Write a strange letter and drop it on the sidewalk

Take a hot shower

Go thrifting

Bake cookies

TO DO *High*

Go body surfing

See an IMAX movie

Write a haiku (see page 156)

Walk through a cemetery

Write a letter to Santa Claus

Write a letter to Mrs. Claus

Watch *Wizard of Oz* synched with Pink Floyd's *Dark Side of the Moon*

Play guitar

Hug a tree

Get a Slinky and go to the largest staircase in your town

Skype a stranger

Watch *Wizard of Oz* synched with *Cheech & Chong's Greatest Hit*

Draw an original comic strip

Eat toast under a comforter, for toasted toasty toast

Go web surfing

Go ocean surfing

Go ghost-hunting

Drink red wine

Invent shit

Watch fireworks

Watch a 3-D movie

Learn card tricks

Take a mellow bike ride

Bash the bishop

Flick the bean

Build a bong

Go to the ocean and count the waves—see how high you can get

Finger paint

Start a web site

Walk deep into the woods and get naked

Talk in slow motion

Go to an aquarium

Redecorate your living room

Draw the perfect cannabis leaf

Turn off the lights and talk with flashlights under your chins

Write a song

Have sex again

Play buzbee

Clean the entire house

Make milkshakes

Bake bread

Visit a chat room

Write a country song

Get lost in an encyclopedia (ok, Wikipedia)

Watch a children's movie

Learn some magic tricks

Play a kazoo

Paint the basement

Eat good chocolate

Arm wrestle

Sit in a hot tub

Have an impromptu talent show

Clean your stoner kit

Make hand shadows on the wall

And a Few Things Not to Do *High*

Tow your friends on a sled behind your car

Minor roofing repairs

Night kayaking

Get straight

Say tongue twisters

Call your family priest

Go to the DMV

Take a cold shower

Walk into a dark basement alone

Ask a cop for directions

CANNABIS STRAINS
Whatever Floats Your Brain
Is it just a coincidence that the number of TV channels to choose from has grown at the same rate as the number of different pot strains out there?

Back in the sixties and seventies, there weren't a whole lot of choices, and that made life less complicated. We had seven or eight TV stations coming through the rabbit ears, and your dealer only ever offered, like, nine varieties of weed, depending on what was around.

Today, there are hundreds if not thousands of strains and hybrids and clones, with so many different names and numbers and sources, and with new ones all the time, that it's hard to keep track. Next time your 420 bike messenger drops in with a box of sealed plastic cubes with white tape labels, be on the lookout for some of our favorite names (listed on the next page). Not that we've tried most of these . . . we just like the handles.

But first, a few lines about the two main types of cannabis—Indica and Sativa. And a note that some of the new strains are hybrids that combine both Indica and Sativa qualities.

INDICA

Indica plants typically grow shorter and wider, and are usually a darker-green color, than Sativa plants. Their buds are dense, thick, and aromatic. Popular Indica strains include Afghani, Blueberry, Kush, Northern Lights, Romulan, and White Rhino.

The buzz you get from an Indica plant tends to be more of a full-body, very relaxed, and soothing high that you will most likely enjoy while completely chilling out and melting into a couch or easy chair.

SATIVA

Sativa plants grow taller and narrower, and are usually a lighter-green color, than Indica plants. They're not as easy to grow indoors because they can reach heights over twenty feet. The aroma and flavor of Sativa ranges from earthy to sweet and fruity. Popular Sativa strains include Haze (several varieties), Jack Herer, Full Moon, African Buzz, Cinderella-99, and Train Wreck.

Since Sativa generally has a higher THC count than Indica, the high you get can be more cerebral, energized, creative, and social, and is probably your better choice if you're going outside the house.

STRAINS OF THE '70S

Acapulco Gold, Panama Red, California Sensimilla, Colombian,
Mexican, Hawaiian, Maui Wowie, Thai Stick, Homegrown
That's all, folks!

STRAINS OF THE 21ST CENTURY

Afghan Delight, Afghani Orange, Afghanica, AK-47, Alpha 13, Amazonia, Ambrosia, Americano, Amnesia 99, Amstel Gold, Amsterdam Bubblegum, Apocalypse, Apollo 11, Apollo 13, Apollo Orange, Apollo's Trip, Apple Pie, Asia Girl, Astroboy, Aurora, Australian Blue, Avalon, B-52, Bahia Black Head, Baked Alaska, Baldy, Bangi, BC Albino Rhino, BC God Bud, BC Sweet Tooth, Beauty and the Beast, Belizian Sativa, Betazoid, Berry Blaster, Berry Bolt, Big Bang, Big Buddha Blue Cheese, Big Funk, Big Mac, Bitchin Blue, Black Bubble, Black Goo, Black Ice, Black Mamba, Black Russian, Blonde Widow, Blue Alaskan, Blue Cheese, Blue Dynamite, Blue Goo, Blue Grape #1, Blue Hen, Blue Moon Rocks, Blue Velvet, Blueberry Magic, Blueberry Punch, Bluez Cluez, BOG BoggleGum, Bottle Rocket, Brains Escape, Brainwreck, Brazillian Skunk, Bubba Kush, Bubblefunk, Buddha, Butterscotch Hawaiian, C4, California Miss, Candy Cane Brain, Canna Sutra, Cannalope Haze, Celestial Temple Sativa, Cheese, Chemota Dragon, Cherry Bomb, Chilla, Chocolate Chunk, Cinderella Blues, Citrus Skunk, City Slicker, Cloud #7, Cotton Candy, Couchlock, Crazy Daze, Cripple Creek, the Crystal Ship, Cujo, Da Bomb, Dankee Doodle, Dark Vader, Daywrecker, Deep Chunk, Devil, Diablo, Diesel 39, Dirty Harry, Doc Chronic, Double Bubble, Durban Thai Highflier, Dutch Dragon, Early Brambleberry, El Peru, Elvis aka Elvis, Euforia, Far Out, Fast Blast, Fig Widow Queen, Fighting Buddha, Five-O, Flo, Fruit Bowl, Fuma Con Diablos, G-Star, General's Daughter, Ghandi, Ghost, God's Treat, Golden Moon, Gonzo #1, Gourdbuster,

Grape Mayhem, Grapeskunk, Great White Shark, Green Giant, Grimm White Shark, Gypsy's Kiss, Hash Balls 2, Haley's Comet, Hardcore, Hawaiian Snow, Haze, Heavy Duty Fruity, Herijuana, the HOG, Hubba Bubba, Ice Queen, Ingemar's Punch, Island Lady, Jack Flash, Jack the Ripper, Jackie O, Janis Special, Jillybean, Jim Dandy, Juicy Fruit, K.C. 42, K-Train, Kahuna, Karpov, Kill Bill, Killer Queen, Kiwi, Kong, Krushage, L.A. Confidential, Lavendar, Lemon Bud, Lifesaver, Lone Ranger, Love Potion #9, Lowrider, Mako Shark, Magic Carpet Ride, Manolito 1, Marley's Collie, Martian Mean Green, Maui Mist, Medicine Man, Merlin's Dream, Mindfuck, Mississippi Queen, Moon Shadow, Moonflower, Morning Dew, Mountain Jam, Mr. Majestyx, Mr. Nice, Neon Super Skunk, Nepalese Grizzly, Neville's Haze, New Purple Power, New York City Diesel, Nirvana Special, No Mercy Special, North #1, Northern Lights, Odin's Hammer, Optimus Prime, Orange Crush, Orange Peako Cambodian, Ortega Indica #1, the Other Cyrstal Ship, Pakalolo, Panama Punch, Passion #1, Peak 19, Pine Tar Kush, Pineapples Punch, Pink Candy, the Pure, Purple Czar, Purple Hippo, Pyramid, Quick Mist Diesel, Raccoon, the Real McCoy, Reclining Buddha, Red Horse, Reefer Madness, Reeferman's Space Queen, RFK, Rock Star, Romulan, Royal Hawaiian, Sabre-Tooth, Schnazzleberry, Señor Garcia, Sensitron, Shanti Devil, Shit, Shiva Shanti II, Shock, Silver Dream, Silverado, Skunk #5, Skunkaberry, Sky Dog, Smoka Cola, Smokey Bear, Southern Lights, Space Queen, Star Chief, Star Gazer, Sticky Sista, Stonehedge, Stoney Baloney, Sudden Impact, Sugar Daddy, Sugar Klingon II, Sunshine Daydream, Super Dawg, Swazi Redbeard, Sweet Dreams, Swiss Miss, Taco, Tanzanian Magic, Thai-Tanic, Thumper, Thunder Fuckin' Wonder, Thunderfuck Diesel, Time Bomb, T.N.T., Top 44, Top Lady, Toxic Blue, Trance, Tribal Vision, Trix, TC Tarantula, Tropical Timewarp, Turtle Power, Uber Candy Haze, Very White, Viet Combo, Viper, Voodoo, Vortex, Waldo, Warlock, White Grizzly, White Rhino, White Tusk, Willie D, Willie Nelson, Wonder 99, Yellow Brick Wall, Zagorsk

And that's just a small percentage, folks!

"Dave's not Here, man"

by Cheech & Chong

(Soft knocks at the door)

CHONG: Who is it?

CHEECH: It's me, Dave. Open up, man, I got the stuff.

(More knocks)

CHONG: Who is it?

CHEECH: It's me, Dave, man. Open up, I got the stuff.

CHONG: Who?

CHEECH: It's, Dave, man. Open up, I think the cops saw me come in here.

(More knocks)

CHONG: Who is it?

CHEECH: It's, Dave, man. Will you open up, I got the stuff with me.

CHONG: Who?

CHEECH: Dave, man. Open up.

CHONG: Dave?

CHEECH: Yeah, Dave. C'mon, man, open up, I think the cops saw me.

CHONG: Dave's not here.

CHEECH: No, man, I'm Dave, man.

(Sharp knocks at the door)

CHEECH: Hey, c'mon, man.

CHONG: Who is it?

CHEECH: It's Dave, man. Will you open up? I got the stuff with me.

CHONG: Who?

CHEECH: Dave, man. Open up.

CHONG: Dave?

CHEECH: Yeah, Dave.

CHONG: Dave's not here.

CHEECH: What the hell? No, man, I am Dave, man. Will you...

(More knocks)

CHEECH: C'mon! Open up the door, will you? I got the stuff with me, I think the cops saw me.

CHONG: Who is it?

CHEECH: Oh, what the hell is it...c'mon. Open up the door! It's Dave!

CHONG: Who?

CHEECH: Dave! D-A-V-E! Will you open up the goddam door!

CHONG: Dave?

CHEECH: Yeah, Dave!

CHONG: Dave?

CHEECH: Right, man. Dave. Now will you open up the door?

CHONG: Dave's not here.

HEMP!

"Make the most of the Indian hemp seed and grow it everywhere."
—GEORGE WASHINGTON

"Hemp is of first necessity to the wealth and protection of the country."
—THOMAS JEFFERSON

To get right to the point, cannabis is the biggest cash crop on Earth today. It's also arguably the most important and useful plant in human history.

The first thing to know about cannabis is that there are two main types of the plant—marijuana and hemp—that look similar but are very different.

"Marijuana" is the word for any cannabis that contains THC (tetrahydrocannabinol).

"Hemp" is the word that describes the non-THC variety of cannabis.

In other words—marijuana gets you high; hemp don't.

But you can use hemp for thousands of other purposes, and humans have used it for centuries all over the world to great benefit. Hemp was one of the first plants to be cultivated by people in their transition from nomadic hunter-gatherers to farmers and then builders of civilizations. Without hemp, you could be sitting on a horse's ass right now riding toward the next hunting grounds hoping to find food, instead of nice and cozy on your couch and wondering what's in the fridge.

Hemp continues to be grown and processed all over the world—except in the United States, which only allows imports of hemp products. People use hemp in oil, seed, and fiber form to generate tens of thousands of products and uses, from fabrics to foods to fuels and other more specific things that begin with letters besides "f" like:

American flags, backpacks, belts, biodegradable plastics, body lotion, books, bracelets, car parts, cardboard, caulk, cereal, coffee, concrete, containers, dog collars, fiberboard, Frisbees, hats, insulation, lip balm, milk, musical instruments, mustard, packaging materials, pants, paper, pet chew toys, plastic bags, plastics, plywood, pretzels, protein shakes, rope, salad dressing, salve, ship sails, shampoo and conditioner, shirts, shoes, sneakers, soap, string, tents, toothbrushes, towels, trail mix, vitamins, wallets, wedding dresses, and even the kitchen sink.

But not in 'Merica! Because growing and manufacturing hemp remains illegal in the good ol' U.S. of A. And don't think that hemp was the baby thrown out with the bathwater when marijuana was made illegal in 1937. The people who passed the Marihuana Tax Act of 1937 knew what they were doing by also including hemp. They were asked to, or told to, by corporations like DuPont, which had developed the synthetic fiber nylon in 1935.

Did you know that there was a time in America when up to ninety percent of all rope, twine, cordage, ship sails, canvas, fiber, and cloth was made out of hemp fiber? And that many of these uses of hemp were replaced in 1937 by DuPont's newly created synthetic fiber, nylon, when hemp became illegal?

If you think about it for a second, you'll understand the rea$on why DuPont and others would have an interest in banning marijuana and hemp.

But the fact is, cannabis doesn't have to remain banned forever, and activists continue to work to right the wrong. Other nations that had banned hemp when they banned marijuana, at the same time the U.S. did, have seen the light and changed their laws, including Canada, the U.K., most European countries, and many more. 'Merica's got to be next.

When you think about it, it is truly insane that Americans have not been able to grow hemp and produce tons of awesome products with it for over seventy-five years now. After all, before 1937, hemp had a long, healthy tradition in America and was its most important and valuable crop, not to mention its most-prescribed drug. And because of its value, it has to be again. Soon.

Hemp in American History

- ❉ It was legal to pay taxes with hemp in America from until the early 1800s

- ❉ Refusing to grow hemp during the seventeenth and eighteenth centuries was against the law

- ❉ George Washington, Thomas Jefferson and other founding fathers grew hemp and fervently sang its praises

- ❉ Benjamin Franklin owned one of the first paper mills in America, which processed hemp

- ❉ The first books, newspapers, maps, and charts made in America were made from hemp

- ❉ Betsy Ross's flag, and the first drafts of the Declaration of Independence and the Constitution, were all made from hemp

- ❉ Abraham Lincoln grew hemp on his farm

- ❉ The first crop grown in many states was hemp

- ❉ Hemp was America's largest legal cash crop until the twentieth century

- ❉ Virtually every U.S. president used cannabis as medication before prohibition

- ❉ In 1916, the U.S. government stated that by the 1940s all paper would come from hemp and that deforestation for paper would end

- Henry Ford's first Model-T was constructed from hemp-plastic panels (whose impact strength is ten times stronger than steel), and was built to run on hemp gasoline

- In the 1930s, hemp had become the first cash crop to exceed a business potential of a billion dollars annually—then the Marihuana Tax Act was passed, and that put an end to that

Hemp Factizoids

- Hemp is among the oldest industries on the planet

- Hemp is one of the most easily absorbed foods by the body, and is extremely healthy in all its many food forms

- Hemp seed is highly nutritious and contains more essential fatty acids than any other food source

- Hemp seed is second only to soybeans in terms of providing complete protein, but it is more digestible than soy

- Hemp has a high vitamin-B level and is rich in cellulose, both very good for the body

- Hemp fibers are among the Earth's longest natural soft fibers, making it extremely useful for countless applications

- Hemp is a fantastic fuel; the hydrocarbons in hemp can be processed into a wide range of biomass energy forms from pellets to liquids to gas, and widespread development of hemp biofuels would significantly decrease our dangerous consumption of dirty fuels like oil, coal, gas, and nuclear power

- Hemp is extremely resistant to insects and disease, and can easily be grown organically without the need for harmful pesticides and fungicides—unlike many other crops

- Hemp grows so fast and wide that it creates a natural canopy that prevents harmful weed growth around it, eliminating the need for dangerous herbicides

- Hemp produces more pulp per acre than trees, and can be used to make any type or quality of paper

- The hemp paper manufacturing process is far better for the environment than that of tree-based paper; it requires less acid for pulping, less chemicals for bleaching, and produces less wastewater contamination

- Hemp paper can be recycled more times than tree-based paper

- Hemp fiberboard is stronger than wood fiberboard

- Hemp can easily replace most petrochemical products (and the pollution and health hazards that come with them), including cellophane, plastics, resins, and a lot more

At this point, you might want to put down the book, pick up the phone, and call your congressman, senator, and president to inform them that you are hip to the reasons why hemp is really illegal, that you believe it is a crime against America for politicians to allow industrial hemp to remain illegal, and to demand that they fix this little mistake, pronto. There's more info later in the book to help you join the fight to legalize it.

Products derived from hemp

THE CASH CROP

Cannabis is the biggest cash crop in the world today. And in America, the value of marijuana revenue each year actually exceeds corn and wheat combined, hard to believe since most cannabis use leads to mass consumption of corn and wheat snack foods.

JUST IMAGINE HOW MUCH REVENUE WEED COULD GENERATE IF IT WAS LEGALLY GROWN AND SOLD AND ITS REVENUE (PICTURED BELOW) WAS TAXED

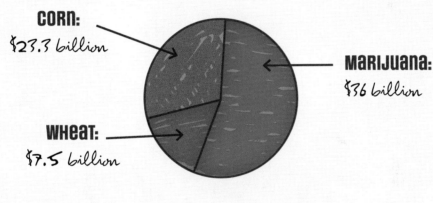

CORN:
$23.3 billion

MARIJUANA:
$36 billion

WHEAT:
$7.5 billion

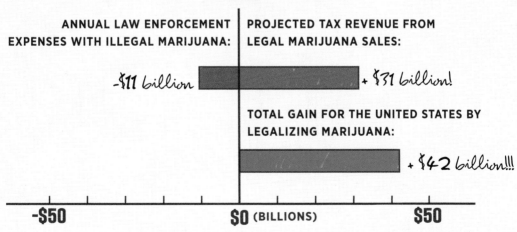

ANNUAL LAW ENFORCEMENT EXPENSES WITH ILLEGAL MARIJUANA:

-$11 billion

PROJECTED TAX REVENUE FROM LEGAL MARIJUANA SALES:

+ $31 billion!

TOTAL GAIN FOR THE UNITED STATES BY LEGALIZING MARIJUANA:

+ $42 billion!!!

-$50 $0 (BILLIONS) $50

STONER KIT

Every stoner has a kit—a box or a container or a drawer or a corner of the floor where you keep your stuff, along with all the stuff you use to smoke your stuff. And when you go away for the weekend, you take an even smaller kit along. If you looked into a typical stoner kit, here's some of the stuff you would probably find.

Home Kit

BOX OR CONTAINER: Like a cigar box or shoebox or lunchbox or old sock

WEED: A few kinds—some Sativa, some Indica, some hybrid

EMPTY BAGGIES: For storing and sharing

ROLLING PAPERS: Two packs of brown papers, one pack of leopard skins

ROLLING MACHINE: Or use a dollar bill

BOWLS: Glass or stone or steel or wood

CHILLUM: For when you want to smoke vertically

DUGOUT AND BAT: Packed with ground weed and ready to travel

SCREENS: Some new ones and a few crusty used ones

LIGHTER: For fire

EXTRA LIGHTERS: Because you really need fire

GRINDER: To grind buds fine

ROACH CLIP: To smoke the bone to the bone

WIRE BRUSH: To brush the screens and tubes

SAFETY PINS: For poking holes in foil, cleaning screens, etc.

SMALL MEDICINE BOTTLES WITH LIDS: For roaches and hash

SCALE: Handheld with roach clip; or small electronic gram scale

LARGE PAPER CLIPS: To clean out bowl and bong

OZIUM: Air freshener

INCENSE: Ditto above

CHEWING GUM: Mouth freshener

EYEDROPS: To get the red out

MEDICAL MARIJUANA DOCTOR'S CERTIFICATE: Except WA and CO

EXTRAS: They won't fit in the kit box, but nearby will be one or more water bongs (glass or plastic), a party bong (e.g. a ceramic skull with six party tubes), a vaporizer, copies of *High Times* magazine, Mason jars for holding bud, a towel (to place under the door), and a sploofer (an empty toilet-paper roll filled with dryer sheets to blow into to kill the smell of your exhale)

Weekender Kit

GROUND WEED: In an opaque medicine bottle

TRAVEL BOWL: Something small, with a sliding lid

AND/OR DUGOUT AND BAT: Packed with ground weed

AND/OR DOOBIES: Stored so they don't get crushed

TINFOIL: To fashion into a small bowl, or to hold roaches

LIGHTER: For fire

GUM: Mouth freshener

EYEDROPS: To get the red out

OZIUM: Air freshener (for vehicular use only)

Day Kit

BUD IN TINFOIL: The tinfoil to be shaped into a bowl when ready to smoke

OR, A COUPLE DOOBIES: If there's a safe place to store without crushing

LIGHTER: For fire

High Ideas

One thing that stoners have in common is the habit of throwing out questions and ideas and concepts and nonsense that make you wonder or laugh or figure out some cosmic truth. Even straight-up questions like "Where's the lighter?" can lead down some interesting paths. Either way, stoner conversation-starters like these are always entertaining; maybe it's the delivery?

KIDS LOVE CLIMBING TREES; WHY DON'T ADULTS?

If there was a wall at the end of the universe, what's on the other side of the wall?

The only thing that will bring peace on Earth is an alien invasion.

Do you have a joint, man?

HOW MUCH MONEY DO YOU HAVE ON YOU?

WHEN YOU STICK OUT YOUR TONGUE, DOES THE AIR GET WET?

What color are these walls?

What's that thing on the table, man?

When marijuana becomes legal I'm going to open a houseboat smoke shop on the Mississippi River.

Have you ever had a near-death experience?

Who's hungry?

Why don't they make a device that instantly translates any language into your language?

What did you just say?

What's up with car-radio remote controls?

IS THE WHOLE POINT OF SOCIETY TO MAKE INDIVIDUALS GET MARRIED TO HAVE CHILDREN AND BUY THEM SHIT?

IF SNAPPING TURTLES WERE PEOPLE, WHAT JOB WOULD THEY HAVE?

Who is the greatest superhero?

Who's more logical, a child or a drunk?

What happens if you use cannabis leaves in compost fertilizer to grow cannabis?

Dr. Seuss was an alien.

That's not a joint, man; that's a toothpick.

WHICH TESTICLE HANGS LOWER - LEFT OR RIGHT?

Who would win a fight between a horse and a deer?

Describe the color blue.

GOD IS DOG SPELLED BACKWARD. HMMMM.

Is it time for another bong hit yet

What did you just say?

Say "ing-ing" until it just sounds like "ing."

Are you gonna finish that?

If you could have one superpower, what would it be?

WHAT IF DEATH WAS LIKE THE LAST PAGE OF *GO, DOG, GO*?

Mellow out, man!

No one is ever alright, because they're always half left.

Where's that Thai stick?

Who am I?

WHERE'S THE LIGHTER?

When you think of cows, do you think "lazy" or "tasty"?

Why was reality during childhood so hazy?

WHERE am I?

Who would win a fight between an alligator and a lion?

A WHOLE UNIVERSE COULD EXIST UNDER YOUR FINGERNAIL.

Why did Custer show up for Custer's last stand?

Was that a cop car?

What would it be like to live inside a smoke bubble?

WHY SHOULD MARIJUANA BE LEGAL?

What if dreams are real and life is just a dream?

Hey look at this thing on my phone.

THE UNIVERSE IS ONE BIG COMPUTER, AND IT WAS PROBABLY PURCHASED AT BEST BUY.

Is this a dream?

Perfectly healthy people in the future are going to replace their arms and legs with bionic limbs.

There are more insects living in your body than there are people on Earth.

DESCRIBE A TIME YOU ALMOST GOT BUSTED.

What time is it again?

Are my eyes red?

Name as many stoner cartoon characters you can think of.

What was I just saying?

What happens if you turn a corkscrew counter-clockwise?

WOULD YOU RATHER HAVE BAD SEX OR A BAD BURRITO?

WHERE DID THAT GUY GO

WHO WAS HERE BEFORE?

What's the name of that song that goes, "Wah waaah . . . bah dah dum; Wah waaah . . . bah dah dah dum; Boo-boo doo-doo boo-doo boo-doo bo dah bah dah ba daaah"?

Do old people give a fuck?

If you could smoke a joint with three people from the past, present or future, who would it be?

What's the sound of one hand clapping?

What am I?

You got any visine?

Say "The sixth sick sheik's sixth sheep's sick."

UFOs aren't aircraft; they're living beings.

IF GIRLS HAVE A G SPOT, DO BOYS HAVE A B SPOT?

Holy shit! Pluto is not a planet anymore!

Is that still lit?

I wish I was a Bonobo monkey.

Do deaf people think in language?

Do stoners in the Southern Hemisphere pass right?

CLOCKWISE FROM TOP LEFT: Global Marijuana March,
High Times Annual Cannabis Cup, Ann Arbor Hash Bash

LET'S PARTY!

A World of Cannabis Festivals

Is there a subculture of people on Earth more inclined to party than the stoner culture? We think not. And it's only natural that many great, big, fun (and important) events have become annual gatherings in spots across the United States and the world. Here's a snapshot of some of the best stoner festivals that are open to all. You. Are. Invited.

Ann Arbor Hash Bash

Originating in 1972 in Ann Arbor, Michigan, this annual festival is held on the campus of the University of Michigan during the first week of April.

The festival is sponsored and planned by NORML (National Organization for the Reform of Marijuana Laws), a registered nonprofit organization, and its focus is on working to reform Michigan's marijuana laws. Among other things.

The first Hash Bash was held on Saturday, April 1, 1972, in response to the March 9, 1972, decision by the Michigan Supreme Court that undid the law that was used to convict cultural activist John Sinclair for possession of two joints, in effect leaving the state without any law prohibiting marijuana use for a few weeks. A new law was in place soon after the April 1 gathering, but the inaugural gathering itself included legal herb smoking due to the calendar glitch!

The festival features a lively menu of speeches, live music, street vendors, and some civil disobedience, all focused on the goal of reforming federal, state, and local marijuana laws.

Global Marijuana March (GMM)

Originating in 1999, this widespread event—also known as the Million Marijuana March (MMM)—now has over 700 participating cities worldwide each year on the first Saturday in May. Events include political marches, rallies, raves, concerts, strategy meetings, festivals, information dispensing, and lots of weed-fueled merriment.

The two main organizers are, from the beginning, accomplished American social activist Dana Beal (cures-not-wars.org), and *Cannabis Culture* magazine (cannabisculture.com).

The main countries with participating cities include Australia, Brazil, Canada, New Zealand, and the United States. And GMM is always willing to take more comers.

Great Midwest Marijuana Harvest Festival

Originating in 1970 in Madison, Wisconsin, and held each year from Thursday-Sunday on the first (usually) weekend of October, this celebration is the longest-running known cannabis festival in the United States.

This festival was conceived in 1970 as an anti-war protest, but soon evolved into a cannabis legalization rally, and has remained so for the last four decades.

The festival includes a Friday evening benefit to kick off the weekend, including numerous live bands, guest speakers, information tables, and all kinds of vending at the Library Mall in Madison, WI. Recently, a silent auction and hemp fashion show were added to the menu of events.

The festival ends with Sunday's traditional Parade to the Capitol for a concert and political rally.

High Times Annual Cannabis Cup

Originating in 1987 in Amsterdam, Netherlands, and held annually during the week of America's Thanksgiving holiday, this is arguably the biggest cannabis event of the year, sponsored and organized by *High Times* magazine.

The Cannabis Cup was founded by Steven Hager a writer, journalist, filmmaker, cannabis activist, and former editor (and current editor emeritus) of *High Times* magazine.

The Cannabis Cup is a five-day-long international celebration of the many wonderful things about marijuana. Its official purpose is to bring cannabis fans and experts together so that they can "taste" and discuss the latest strains of marijuana and hashish.

The main event at the festival pulls together judges from around the world to sample and vote for their favorite marijuana varieties. These judges decide the ultimate winner of the Cannabis Cup, best new product, best booth, best glass, and best hash. And a team of VIP judges decide which seed company has grown the best marijuana.

The festival is open to the public. Bring a lighter.

LOS ANGELES MILLION MARIJUANA MARCH

Originating in 1998 in Los Angeles, California, this festival is held each year during the first weekend of May in Leimert Park. It is part of the GMM.

The LA Million Marijuana March is a two-day celebration featuring concerts and speaker events focused on efforts to educate the public with the goal of legalizing marijuana, not only for medical marijuana, but for recreational use as well.

NIMBIN MARDIGRASS

Originating in 1993 in Nimbin, New South Wales, Australia, the popular gathering takes place each year during the first weekend of May, and is a participant in the Global Marijuana March.

The MardiGrass is basically a rally to reform cannabis law and to celebrate marijuana. It features peaceful protest and parades meant to focus on the problems with illegality and prohibition, and to promote growing and using marijuana plants.

MardiGrass' main event is the Hemp Olympix, which includes competitions like Joint Rolling, Bong Throw and Yell, and Growers Ironperson events.

It also includes the Nimbin Cannabis Cup, Harvest Ball, and Picker's Ball, with live music and dance parties.

Annual attendees always look forward to seeing "The Big Joint" (made from large bed sheets) and the dancing "Ganja Faeries," girls dressed as green fairies—the unofficial mascots of the Nimbin MardiGrass.

TORONTO FREEDOM FESTIVAL

Originating in 1998 in Toronto, Canada, the festival is held annually in Queen's Park during the first weekend of May. It's also a part of the GMM.

The Toronto Freedom Festival is co-organized by Gabe Simms, a prominent activist in Toronto, Canada. In just over thirteen years, it has become a complete sensation. Today, the festival draws 30,000 likeminded marijuana lovers, cannabis-legalization activists, and pot-friendly vendors who gather to have fun and to promote responsible legalization of marijuana in Canada.

SEATTLE HEMPFEST

Originating in 1991 in Seattle, Washington, and originally called the Washington Hemp Expo, this major event takes place annually in downtown Seattle during the third weekend of August.

While their website (hempfest.org) describes the event as a "humble gathering of stoners," this event has become arguably the world's largest annual gathering to advocate decriminalization of marijuana and to celebrate stoner culture.

The Seattle Hempfest is a three-day event, with a political rally, concert, and arts and crafts

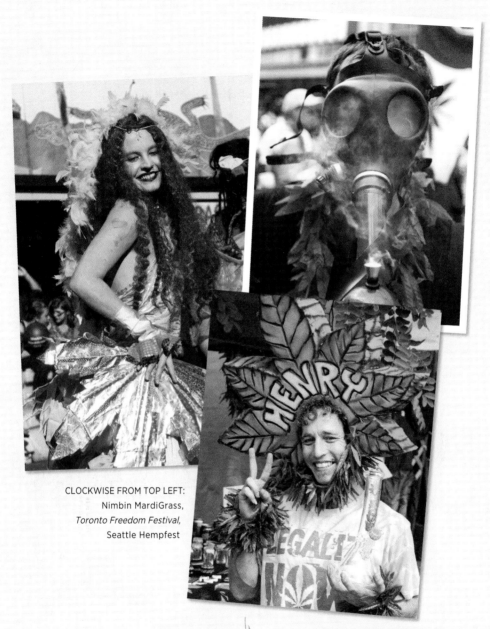

CLOCKWISE FROM TOP LEFT:
Nimbin MardiGrass,
Toronto Freedom Festival,
Seattle Hempfest

fair, and typically draws attendance numbers over a quarter-million people. It has a budget of over half a million dollars to operation, but admittance to the general public is totally free.

There logistics include no less than five stages for speakers and musical performances.

Notable Hempfest speakers in 2011—believe it or not—featured a number of elected officials, including Seattle Mayor Mike McGinn, City Attorney Pete Holmes, and Washington State Representatives Mary Lou Dickerson and Roger Goodman.

STONER TOOLS OF THE TRADE

When a stoner is lucky enough to score a bag of weed,
the next step is deciding how to smoke it. The good thing is,
you got options with this variety of paraphernalia.

JOINT

Is there anything more perfect than a joint? It's portable. It lights fast and stays lit. It can accommodate anywhere from two to eight people. It smells nice. And it gets you high! With all the various apparatus available (see below), the good ol' joint is still very popular and will always remain a good option. And if you want to jazz it up, try leopard or zebra skins.

CHILLUM

Chillums are like pipes, but instead of the bowl being turned on a ninety-degree angle, it simply is built into the end opposite the mouthpiece. Personally, we prefer pipes because with chillums, you have to sort of hold the piece upright and crick your neck to get a hit. But if you're offering, we're accepting!

PIPE (OR BOWL)

Just as commonly used as the joint, pipes are great because they're compact, travel well, are easy to use, can accommodate a small group, and come in all kinds of cool designs and media from glass to wood to metal to rock to plastic. Just don't forget the screens.

BONG

There may not be two more exciting words in the English language when used together than "Bong Hit!" Bongs give you the most bang for your buck of any smoking device. The keys are that they're bigger than pipes and can produce and hold more smoke, and they contain a water chamber through which the smoke passes, cooling it considerably and allowing your body to inhale a lot more of it, while also removing many impurities and carcinogens. As many people say, "One bong hit and I'm good." For about thirty minutes, that is.

HOOKAH

Hookah, lookah, doopity, doo, I've got another method for you. The hookah is basically a fancy party bong, originally developed in Persia around the sixteenth century for smoking sweet-flavored tobaccos, that has been co-opted by some stoners for use with sweet-flavored marijuana.

PARTY BONG

A party bong has the same technical qualities of a bong, with one added bonus—instead of one opening to draw smoke from, it can have anywhere from two to eight tubes coming out of the chamber so that many people can toke together. They also come in awesome designs, like skulls and dragon heads with LED lights in the eye sockets. The only drawback to using a party bong is that, during a hit, it's hard not to burst out laughing while looking at your friends doing all they can to suck in a big one. And there's no worse buzzkill than guffawing during a blast and losing all that precious smoke!

DUGOUT AND BAT

Also known as a "one-hitter," a dugout is a small wooden container, shaped sort of like a smaller cigarette box, that has one large chamber for ground weed, and a narrow round chamber to hold the "bat," which is a hollow metal or glass tube about the size of a cigarette, with a mouthpiece on one end and an opening on the opposite end for the weed. To use, dig the bat into the weed chamber until the end fills with stuff. Then light and draw. Great for travel, or for when you just need a quick pick-me-up.

VAPORIZOR

You gotta love technology, and the vaporizer is the apex of stoner technology. Developed by "Eagle Bill" Wood and introduced at the 1994 Cannabis Cup, the beauty of the vaporizer is that it uses a heating element (not fire) to extract THC from cannabis, producing the exact same high as burning weed, but offering many positive developments in health, stealth, and wealth.

HEALTH. Since no organic matter is burned, you are inhaling vapor, not smoke. According to studies by the University of California, San Francisco, vaporizing produces "virtually no exposure to harmful combustion products" such as tar, and extremely reduced emission of carbon monoxide.

STEALTH. Exhaled vapor is much stealthier than the lingering reek of pot smoke, as it produces far less odor, and it dissipates much faster than burned weed.

WEALTH. Because vaporizers extract THC with greater efficiency than burning it, you use almost half the amount of marijuana to get high, saving buko bucks.

There's a lot to love about vaporizers, so look into them and ask for one for Christmas.

EAT IT!

If you don't want to inhale burning organic matter via smoking, and you have no vaporizer, or you just prefer the different kind of high that comes from digesting THC, your option is to open wide and eat it! See page 99 for instructions on how to make a peanut butter firecracker.

IMPROVISED PIPES, BOWLS, AND BONGS

If you don't have papers, or a proper pipe, or a chillum, or a bong, or a vaporizer, or some peanut butter, or any friends who have any of the above, you still got options! Not only is it very easy to make a pipe or a bowl or a bong or even a deluxe "gravity bong" from scratch, these improvised tools work almost as good as the real thing. You can use tinfoil, aluminum cans, apples, and other stuff. Turn to page 100 for the lowdown.

Stoner Etiquette

Smoking weed is usually a social thing stoners do with friends and strangers at home, parties, tailgates, concerts, strangers' homes, strangers' vans, festivals, what have you. To do it right, you follow the rules of etiquette that are common knowledge to all stoners.

1. If it's your weed or joint, tell others what it is and whether there's tobacco mixed in.

2. Always grind your weed before packing or rolling.

3. Whoever brings the weed gets the first hit; and if someone else rolled it, they go second.

4. When you light a bowl, light the corner to leave fresh weed on the other side.

5. Don't slobber saliva all over the doob or pipe.

6. Always pass clockwise, to your left.

7. Don't Bogart the joint—puff, puff, then pass.

8. Announce when a bowl gets cashed on your hit.

9. If sharing a bong, don't pass until you've cleared out all the smoke.

10. Always ask before lighting up in someone's house or car.

11. Never smoke someone's weed without asking, or knowing it's ok.

12. Always share with friends and fellow stoners.

13. It's okay to humbly ask other stoners to toke you up if you're dry.

14. Don't "accidentally" pocket someone else's lighter or papers or pipe.

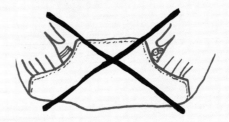

A Trip to
THE HEAD SHOP

Head shops are the most fun anyone can have in a retail store. It's the place to go to stock up on all the paraphernalia and accoutrements that a stoner could ever possibly need, like blacklight posters, bongs, Cheech and Chong posters, crystals, flavored tobaccos, Frisbees, Grateful Dead posters, herb grinders, hackey sacks, hemp wallets, Hendrix posters, incense, jewelry, knickknacks, lighters, one-hitters, pipes, rolling machines, rolling papers, pipes, scales, scrapers, screens, stash boxes, stickers, tee shirts, whippits, and more.

Just make sure you refrain from using any words that have anything to do with anything illegal! By law, head shop owners and employees will have to kick you out of the store if you so much as suggest that they're dealing with anything that promotes illegal activity.

The cryptic conversations that happen in head shops are always interesting and comical. Like this typical tête-á-tête between a customer and clerk:

CLERK: Hello there.

CUSTOMER: Hi . . . lo to you, too. *[Relieved to quickly turn Hi into Hello.]*

CLERK: Can I help you?

CUSTOMER: Yes, I need a couple things. I'm interested in a . . . in one of those, uh, glass things there. *[Points to shelf with bongs.]*

CLERK: Excellent. We have a great selection of water pipes.

CUSTOMER: Yes, water pipes. How about that one there, on the end. *[Points to ceramic skull party bong with six smoking tubes. Clerk takes it down and puts it on the countertop.]*

CLERK: Great choice. This is made by a company called Homegrown.

CUSTOMER: *[Stammering]* Home . . . uh . . . sounds good. It looks pretty intricate. Where do you put the, uh . . . where does the, um, *[purposely muffled word]* go?

CLERK: Your tobacco *[customer almost laughs]* goes in this chamber here, and your filtering water goes in the other chamber opening.

CUSTOMER: Nice, I'll take it. I also need a one-hi- . . . um, a . . . one of those things . . . it's a small wooden box that holds tobacco and comes with a small tube-like, um, for the. . . .

CLERK: You mean a dugout?

CUSTOMER: *[Surprised that he can say "dugout."]* Yes, of course, a dugout. Do you have any?

CLERK: *[Pulls a one-hitter out of a display case.]* Just this one. *[Opens the lid and pulls out the metal bat, which is painted to look like a cigarette.]*

CUSTOMER: Cool! That would fool anyone! *[Clerk looks at customer funny.]* I mean, um, I'm trying to cut back on cigarettes, and, uh, I can just take one puff of tobacco at a time and it still looks like I'm having a full cig. *[Customer almost hyperventilates, averts eye contact with clerk.]*

CLERK: Yes, exactly, that's what dugouts are for. *[Customer laughs nervously.]*

CUSTOMER: I'll take it. And I just need one more thing. *[Hears door open, turns to see a girl with two dogs walk in, turns back.]* Well, uh, we want to make our own, um, whipped cream, and need those things you use to, uh. . . .

CLERK: Whippets!

CUSTOMER: *[Shocked and delighted]* You're allowed to call them whippits?!!

CLERK: *[Bends down to pet the dogs that just ran around the counter.]* Well that's what they are, although some people mistake them for greyhounds. *[Pets the two whippet dogs for a second before they run back around the counter.]* Now what else did you need? Oh, right, you want some N_2O cartridges for making whipped cream. They come a dozen per box. Okay?

CUSTOMER: *[About to pass out]* Yes. N_2O cartridges. That will be all.

CLERK: *[After completing the transaction]* Don't forget your free pouch of cherry tobacco to go with your new water pipe. *[Points to a basket near the door filled with small complimentary pouches of cherry tobacco.]*

CUSTOMER: *[After momentary confusion]* Oh, right. Thanks? *[Takes packet, exits, drops packet in wastebasket just outside door, which is filled with pouches of cherry tobacco.]*

LET'S Make a Dope Deal

by Cheech & Chong

HOST: And now its time for America's favorite daytime fun show...Let's Make a Dope Deal! Let's make a dope deal, where young pushers try to parlay their stash and jump up in the dealerhood. And our first contestant today on Let's-make-a-dope-deal is the former head of the philosophy department at Harvard University. He is the holder of a PhD., an M.A., a B.A., and is a BMF besides, would you please give a big warm welcome for...Bob Bixon! Well, it's really great to have you on the show tonight, Bob. How're you doing?

BOB: Bitchin'

HOST: Bitchin'. Isn't that far out? Solid. Right on, Bob. Tell us, Bob, here's the question I ask of all our contestants: What made you drop out?

BOB: A lot of people think it was the 400 acid trips I took, ya know?

HOST: Uh huh. But, what was it really, Bob?

BOB: One day I played Black Sabbath at 78 speed.

HOST: Then what happened?

BOB: I saw God.

HOST: You saw God. Well, my goodness. That sounds like true enlightenment to me. Now, tell me, Bob, what have you been doing with all those degrees? I noticed you had a PhD., an M.A., a B.A. What have you been doing with all that knowledge?

BOB: Making candles, man.

HOST: Making candles. Well that sounds creative, Bob. What kind of candles are they?

BOB: They're really neat table candles, you know?

HOST: Table candles?

BOB: Yeah, you pour wax on the table.

HOST: Uh huh.

BOB: And you set it on fire, man.

HOST: Well...that sounds like a hot item, Bob. You ready to play our game?

BOB: Yeah

HOST: Ok, you know the rules, you get funded with a stash of 50 keys and you can wager part of them or just some of them on any of our tests.

BOB: 50 keys?

HOST: 50 keys.

BOB: Can I quit now?

HOST: No, no, not yet, Bob, you have to play our game. Ok, Bob, how many you want to wager on the first test?

BOB: All of them.

HOST: All of them! He's going to shoot the works! Or mainline as we call it here on Let's Make a Dope Deal. Ok, Bob, for 50 keys, What is your name? You have 60 seconds.

BOB: Hey, I know that one.

HOST: Starts with a B

BOB: What is it man?

HOST: Ends with a B

BOB: Oh, no, don't tell me.

HOST: Ten seconds, Bob.

BOB: BOB!

HOST: Bob! And you win 50 keys and the tensions mount here on Let's Make a Dope Deal. Oh boy, Bob, now you have 100 keys.

BOB: I almost missed that one.

HOST: Almost did. Ok, here we go, the second one. How many you want to wager this time?

BOB: All of them.

HOST: All of them! He's going to shoot the works again, huh! What balls he has. Ok, here we go, Bob. For another 100 keys. How many joints are in a lid? 30 seconds.

BOB: I know that one.

CROWD 1: 2

CROWD 2: 2?

CROWD 1: I roll big joints.

HOST: Our judges say that's ok. They roll big joints too and you win another 100 keys.

Bob, Host, and crowd all talk at the same time, unclear what is being said

HOST: Ok, now we're going for the big and final test. Ok, in front of you, you see three doors, marked: Door #1, Door #2, Door #3. Behind one of those doors lies 50 pounds of Lebanese blond hash.

BOB: Woahhh.

HOST: Makes your eyes red just thinkin' about them, huh? Ok, Bob, I'm going to make you a deal. I'm going to give you 50 dollars and 50 reds for your keys right now.

Crowd: I'll take the reds!

HOST: I'll give you 1,000 dollars and 50 reds.

BOB: I want the hash.

HOST: He wants the hash! Ok, Bob, here we go, now behind the other two doors are Narcs. Ok, here we go. What'll it be? Will it be door #1, door #2 or...

BOB: Or what?

HOST: Narcs there's two narcs behind the other doors.

BOB: I'll take the reds, man.

HOST: I'm sorry, Bob, it's too late. You have to choose. What'll it be? 1, 2 or 3.

BOB: 4

HOST: No, no, Bob, there's only 3. Oh it's ok, you're nervous, 1, 2, or 3?!

BOB: 2, 1, Ohh number...3.

HOST: 1, 2 or 3?

BOB: 3, no, 1...ahhh. 1, 1.

HOST: You chose door #1, lets see what's behind that door. That's Officer O'Malley, the FBI, You're busted! Join us next week when we play, Let's Make a Dope Deal!

BOB: What happened, man?

THE MAN

Cops and Narcs

The Road Runner had Wile E. Coyote. Sherlock Holmes had Professor Moriarty. God has Satan. And stoners have The Man—a.k.a. Cops, Pigs, Fuzz, Johnny Law, and what have you.

Until marijuana becomes legal everywhere, stoners have to do all they can to stay one step ahead of cops, narcs, the DEA, and any other federale who would just loooooove to confiscate their weed and give them a police record.

You gotta be careful out there. You just never know who might be lurking nearby, ready to insert themselves into your situation and turn your beautiful day into a bust and a buzzkill. But narcs are not as smart as they think they are. If you follow some simple rules, and if you look close enough for a combination of dead giveaways, you'll be safe not sorry.

SIMPLE RULES

* Never deal with someone you don't know.

* Don't assume that if you ask if someone's a cop, they have to tell you. A cop might say what he's gotta say, and lie in court later.

* Never assume that if a guy smokes some weed with you it means he's not a cop. Cops can do drugs while on the job.

* If you sense someone is a narc, clam up and bail.

DEAD GIVEAWAYS

AGE. Narcs are often older than the group they're trying to bust, yet try to look younger, and try too hard.

BASEBALL CAP. Always fitted, often in rally position.

GRATEFUL DEAD TEE SHIRT. Especially a brand new one.

SHORT BEARD. Cops can't grow long beards; they often have to testify in court, and always shave for those appearances.

FAKE MUSTACHE. A common ploy for undercovers; not hard to tell.

DIRTY CLOTHES. Dealers aren't necessarily dirtbags; narcs are, for effect.

FANNY PACK. It's stereotypical but true. (And besides, whether he's a narc or not, do you really want anything to do with a guy who wears a fanny pack?)

TERMINOLOGY. Slang terms are sometimes slightly off, as if he's trying too hard.

BUSYBODY. You see the narc approaching other people before he approaches you.

STANDS TOO CLOSE TO YOU. So your words can be picked up on his recording device.

ACTS HIGH OR DRUNK. Over-acts, that is. You can tell.

THEIR FRIEND. There's always a partner, and the partner always walks up, and they always act like they don't know each other. Pay attention to signs that they are too familiar.

TOO MUCH TOO SOON. Any stranger who sidles up to you and says he knows where to score bud right off the bat—or asks if you do—is a bit off.

TIME CHECK. Beware those who talk too much; most dealers and buyers just want to get in and get out.

CAPTAIN OBVIOUS. Anyone asking a lot of obvious questions should raise a flag.

WHEELS. Don't deal with any-one who drives a Grand Marquis or Impala.

HONEY TRAP. A babe narc. Not sure what to tell you with this type of narc; gets us every time.

Roll, Roll, Roll a Joint

The joint—or doobie, or blunt, or fun stick, or toothpick, or whatever you like to call it—is still one of the most common ways to smoke the ganja. As every stoner knows, not every stoner is what you would call "good" at rolling doobs. But anyone can learn.

The Options

One might say a joint is "a smooth long cylinder of marijuana wrapped in thin smoking paper that tapers slightly at either end and looks like a little white torpedo of fun." And they would be right. But there are also other kinds of specialty joints that people talk about, like the "Cross Joint" which is made of three joints joined together; the "Cone" which is thinner on one end and thicker on the other; the "Tulip" which uses extra papers to create the look of a flower; the "Diamond" which has two joints on either end of a four-jointed diamond shape; the "Secret Agent" which looks like a standard tobacco cigarette; and others. You can find out how to roll all of those styles and more on the internet. But not here! We're here to make sure you just know how to roll what we call a standard fatty. In other words, a joint.

What Makes a J a Good J?

There are a few key elements that make a good quality joint:

* Thick with a consistent amount of herb throughout

* The herb is ground, not in bud form, when rolled

* Not too tight, and definitely not too loose

* Pulls easy with every hit from start to finish

* Maintains its shape throughout the session

* No weed is wasted in the rolling or the smoking

* Doesn't canoe at any point

Step-by-Step

Here's how to slap a fatty together:

1. Always roll above a clear flat surface that can collect excess weed that might fall out while you're rolling.

2. Use good papers, such as rice or hemp.

3. Get some good quality marijuana!

4. Remove all stems and seeds from your weed.

5. Grind the weed so there are no remaining chunks of bud.

6. Take a rolling paper (which typically comes center-folded horizontally in the package) and fold the bottom half (without the glue strip) in half again so the bottom edge touches along the center crease; this creates an area for the weed to settle into, stopping at the lip you created across the bottom.

7. Holding the paper in one hand, sprinkle the weed into the newly creased area.

8. Using your other hand, flatten the weed evenly along the length of the paper.

9. Prepare to roll.

10. Lay the bottom of the weed-filled paper horizontally across the sides of both index fingers, with thumbs positioned on the bottom of the lip.

11. Starting at the center, use both thumbs to gently but firmly roll the paper over the weed in a slight back-and-forth motion to shape the weed into a round tube inside the paper, gradually moving from the center to the ends.

12. When the weed is firmly in shape, and evenly distributed, finish rolling all the way until the glue strip has been wrapped over the joint, the pull back the strip, lick it lightly across its length, and make your final wrap to secure the wet glue strip to the paper, making sure the joint is tight, but not too tight.

13. Tap the ends lightly to prevent any weed from falling out.

14. Let it sit for a few minutes until the glue dries. Voilà!

By George!
Rolling with Money

No matter how many times they read the instructions above, some people just can't roll a spiff spliff with their fingertips—they need some assistance. If you don't have a store-bought rolling machine, the next best rolling machine is sponsored, you might say, by George Washington—it's the good old dollar bill. This method works perfectly every time, even for someone who's all thumbs.

The instructions are just about the same as the steps on page 92, with a few minor tweaks. At Step 6, you want to leave the rolling paper as is—no need to add a crease. At Step 7, instead of putting the pot in the paper, fold the dollar bill in half horizontally and feed the weed into that crease. Perform Steps 10 and 11 with the weed in the bill, not the paper. And at Step 12, once the weed is firmly in shape, simply slide your rolling paper (glue side up and facing you) behind the cylinder of weed, fold the dollar bill closed, and continue rolling the bill until you see the rolling paper completely cover the weed and look like a joint. Next, slide the joint out of the bill, lick the glue strip, and press it closed.

SIZE MATTERS

Everyone rolls their doobies differently. Some people—hopefully no one we know—like to twist up pencil-thin little numbers; we call these folks conservationists, or "cheap." And other dudes twist up two-fisters big enough to turn on every guy in Parliament-Funkadelic, Sly and the Family Stone, Santana, and the Doobie Brothers all at the same time. For the roller in you, or the twister in your crew, here's a handy-dandy sizing chart.

Toothpick

Small

Large

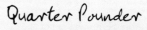
Quarter Pounder

MERIT BADGES

Everyone needs a little recognition every now and then—even stoners. Here are the internationally accepted (we think) symbols of stoner excellence, formed into badges that can be cut out and presented to those friends of yours who deserve to be rewarded for their merits in the various areas of stonerhood. For stoners, it's the next best thing to being knighted.

RELIABLE DEALER   **WEED PROCURER**   **VENUE PROVIDER**   **POT CLEANER**

JOINT ROLLER   **BONG FILLER**   **FIRE STARTER**   **JOINT PASSER**

CANNABIS CONNOISSEUR   **MUNCHIE SUPPLIER**   **COP DETECTOR**   **REALITY CHECKER**

Eat It!

Sometimes you just don't want to smoke, but you do want to get high. Maybe you got a sore throat. Or maybe you're recovering from a broken bone or other illness (ingesting any kind of smoke inhibits healing). Or maybe you don't have a vaporizer yet. Or maybe you can't find a lighter. Or maybe you want to try another kind of high. So what do you do?

Eat it, man!

There are entire cookbooks filled with recipes for cooking cannabis into foods. And we're not just talking about the old standard—hash brownies. There are recipes for adding Vitamin THC to everything from pasta to pizza to French toast to damned-if-we-know.

But really, the only two recipes you need to easily consume your kush via the old piehole, are cannabis ghee and the firecracker. Cannabis ghee is basically condensed butter with THC in it, and Firecrackers are basically homemade peanut-butter crackers with THC in them.

Cooking school is now in session.

CANNABIS GHEE

INGREDIENTS:

- 2 lb. unsalted butter
- 1 ounce finely ground marijuana

DIRECTIONS:

1. Melt the butter in a pan at a low to medium temperature until the butter is hot enough to boil, but not a rolling boil.
2. When froth forms on the surface of the melted butter, remove it with a spoon and toss.
3. Continue until no more froth appears.
4. Store in an airtight container in the refrigerator until it hardens.
5. Place the ghee in a pan on low heat until it begins to simmer. (Note: Do not let the ghee boil or burn; it should only simmer with little or no bubbles.)
6. Add the cannabis slowly, stirring often.
7. Allow to simmer on low heat for an hour.
8. Strain the contents of the pan through cheese cloth, and allow to cool.
9. Store in an airtight container in the refrigerator.

TO USE:

You can use cannabis ghee the same way you use butter. Start with about one-half of a teaspoon on a piece of toast, or on popcorn, or when frying eggs, or any other way you use butter. If you don't get the high you seek, you can gradually increase the dose the next time you use it by one-half teaspoon.

THE FIRECRACKER

INGREDIENTS/TOOLS:

- 10 saltine crackers (or any other kind of cracker; the bigger the better)

- Natural peanut butter or Nutella (name-brand processed PB with hydrogenated oils don't work as well)

- A pile of finely ground weed

DIRECTIONS:

I. Spread peanut butter liberally onto the center of one side of each of the ten crackers, but not all the way to the edges.

2. Carefully sprinkle a quarter-sized pile of finely ground weed on top of the peanut butter on five of the crackers.

3. Take the other five crackers, and press them down very gently on top of the five crackers with the weed, creating five little fortified peanut-butter sandwiches.

4. Place the sandwiches on a plate, and microwave at three-quarter power for exactly 14 seconds.

5. Individually wrap each of the sandwiches in tinfoil, and place all on a cookie sheet into a pre-heated oven at 320-degrees.

6. Cook for 20 minutes exactly. DO NOT OVERCOOK!

7. Remove, allow to cool, then enjoy.

TO USE:

Eat one cracker.

Note: Eating marijuana—whether it's with cannabis ghee or firecrackers—will not get you high instantly the way smoking and vaporizing does. You won't start to feel the effects until at least thirty minutes pass, and maybe not until an hour or more has gone by—everybody's body is different. But you will experience—so say many fans of this format—a much deeper, fuller-body, and trippier high that lasts for hours. So put on your apron and get in the kitchen.

   Bone appetite!

BUILD A BONG! OR A PIPE

Necessity is the mother of invention.

And if you're lucky enough to score a bag of weed, but don't have rolling papers, a bowl, a bong, a vaporizer, or any other paraphernalia, don't worry—you're not out of luck yet. Just get your MacGyver on and try one of these quick classic examples of stoner ingenuity that kicks in when necessity hits.

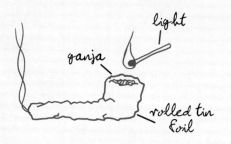

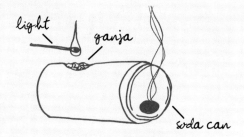

TINFOIL PIPE

The easiest homemade smoking device. Take a rectangular piece of tinfoil the length of an ink pen and several inches wide, wrap it lengthwise around a pen to create a hollow cylinder, remove the pen, bend one end up about two inches from the end to create the bowl, and you're good to go.

ALUMINUM CAN BOWL

Clean out any aluminum can, like a soda or beer can. Lay the can on its side with the mouth opening at 12 o'clock. Press down on the side of the can furthest away from the mouth opening—the idea is to create a small indentation for the bowl. In the middle of the indentation, use a pin or other sharp narrow object to poke a bunch of small holes, big enough for smoke to get through, but small enough that weed doesn't go through. Spark it up!

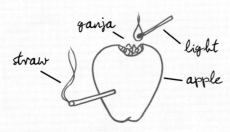

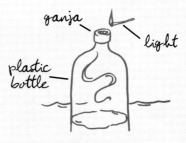

APPLE PIPE

You'll need an apple (pick a hard, non-mushy one), and a pencil or knife. Remove the stem— this is where the bowl will be. Take the pencil and bore it down into the apple from the stem; stop when the tip reaches the center. The hole should be about as thick as your pinkie. Next, bore the pencil into the side of the apple (doesn't matter where you start) until the tip reaches the hollowed center; you'll feel it. Next, blow through the side hole until you feel air come through the top. Let the apple dry for a little bit, or apply some fire to it if you're in a rush. Place a small bud, not shake, into the bowl, and light her up. When done, go ahead and eat that apple. Or toss it. Just don't put it in your stash box for next time.

BONG

We lied in the heading of this section. We're not going to tell you how to build a bong, because it's too complicated—you'd need to have a drill, a downstem, some grommets, and a bunch of free time—and our goal is to get you where you need to be, quickly. But we can tell you how to make a quick "gravity bong". . . .

GRAVITY BONG

This will be the biggest bong hit you've ever done.

TOOLS: A plastic bottle (32- or 64-ounce) with screw-on lid, a knife, a pin, a small piece of aluminum foil, and a kitchen sink filled with water.

INSTRUCTIONS: Remove the lid and use the knife to bore a hole in its center, about the size of your pinkie. Tear off a square of foil about an inch wider than the lid all around. Mold the foil so that the center becomes the bottom of a cone shape. Gently push the bottom of the foil cone into the hole in the lid, from the outside (not the inside where the threads are)—the idea is to create a bowl where the weed goes. Turn the lid upside down and press it on a table so the foil stays in place. Next, take a pin and very carefully poke five or six small holes in the foil bowl, making sure the holes aren't wide enough for weed to fall through. Then cut off the very bottom of the bottle. Fill the sink with water. Fill the bowl with weed. Push the bottle, bottom-side down, down into the water, stopping before the top reaches the water. Then, screw on the lid with the weed in it (note: if you screw on the lid before you put the bottle in the water, the weed will shoot out). Flick your lighter and put the fire on the weed as you slowly pull the bottle up out of the water. When smoke fills the bottle, unscrew the cap, put your lips around the lid, push the bottle back down into the water, and be prepared for a huge rush of smoke into your lungs!

Amsterdam!

Amsterdam, in the Netherlands, is known for many things. Its great museums. Its lovely canals. Its beautiful tulips. Its red-light district.

But ask anyone—non-stoners too—the first thing that comes to mind when you say Amsterdam, and just about everyone will say, Stoner Utopia.

Every stoner dreams of taking a trip to Amsterdam at least once in their life (or at least before weed becomes legal in their state). For half a century, it's been the only city on Earth where a stoner could comfortably get high in a public place knowing they won't face any heat from the police. Stoners make pilgrimages to Amsterdam from all over the world just to be part of the one-of-a-kind stoner scene and to see what it feels like to taste weed freedom.

If you make the pilgrimage, here are some keys to key in on:

LEGALITY. Not to let the truth get in the way of a good story, but the truth is, marijuana isn't really legal in Amsterdam. It's a misdemeanor to possess weed, and illegal to sell it. But don't worry! A non-enforcement policy that has been in effect for decades allows lots of "coffee shops" to sell lots of pot to customers who can smoke it on site and take it to go. The policy has created such a precedent that, on the rare occasion that law enforcement does try to bust someone, the courts always rule against the government and for the stoner. Sounds like Utopia to us.

GRAB A MAP. With almost as many canals as streets, it's not an easy place to find your way around if you're a newcomer, or if you're high and mapless.

COFFEE SHOPS. This is why you're here. The term "coffee shop" in Amsterdam refers to the 200-plus purveyors of pot that also sell coffee, drinks (no alcohol), and food. It's always fun to be in a public café with full marijuana menus, samples to eyeball and smell, free rolling papers in dispensers on tabletops, and lots of mellow happy faces.

PUBLIC SMOKING. Since marijuana is technically illegal in Amsterdam, it's best not to light up in public places, and if you do, be discreet.

MAKING FRIENDS. Weeding out the stoners from non-stoners in most places means asking cryptic questions and dropping subtle hints. In Amsterdam, just walk into a coffee shop and you're guaranteed that everyone is an ally and potential new buddy.

CANNABIS CUP. The greatest gathering on the global stoner social calendar every year is the Cannabis Cup—an incredible, gigantic event that takes place the week of America's Thanksgiving. Started by *High Times* magazine in 1987, it includes five days of parties, rallies, competitions, and much more.

FRIENDLY HOTELS. Many hotels—and even some youth hostels—allow toking in their lobbies, rooms, bars, everywhere! Do a little research before you go, in order to find the right room.

RIJKSMUSEUM. Get high and wander through one of the greatest art museums on Earth, near downtown Amsterdam.

CANNABIS MUSEUM. Get high and wander through the only museum on the planet devoted to your favorite plant, near downtown Amsterdam.

CANALS. Take at least one canal-boat ride while in the "Venice of the North."

RED-LIGHT DISTRICT. Taking a stroll through the famous Amsterdam red-light district is another must-do. And if you got a few extra Euros on you, who knows—you might get lucky.

THAT'S NOT POT!

Plants that Look Like Cannabis But Aren't

When you're out hiking with some stoner friends and you come upon a field that apparently is filled with marijuana plants, make sure you make sure they're actually the THC-filled *Cannabis sativa* plant and not some doppelganger. Because there are actually a lot of impostors out there that share many of the same physical features of pot, but none of the same psychological features, if ya know what I mean. And why wouldn't there be copycat plants? After all, if you were a plant, wouldn't you want to be a pot plant? Here's a field guide to some of the best marijuana mimics in nature.

Japanese Maple

Stinging Nettle

False Aralia

Scarlet hibiscus

Kenaf

Texas Star Hibiscus

Jatropha Multifida

Cleome

Passiflora caerulea

Horseweed

Sawtooth coriander

Flowering blue wild lupin

Castor bean plant

Dotted horsemint

Chaste tree

THE MUNCHIES!

One of the most overcooked stereotypes about stoners is that, after they get stoned, they get a mad appetite and eat everything and anything in sight. Generally speaking, when it comes to stereotyping, it's just not fair to lump a whole group together and say that every individual in the group does this or that. Unless you're talking about stoners and the munchies, then it's completely fair. They will eat anything—brand name, homemade, or a hybrid of the two. They even make a quick snack while waiting for the other snack to finish. And with the creative jolt that pot adds to anything you do, the combinations for munchies are endless.

On the menu tonight and every night. . . .

✳ *Cheetos* ✳ DORITOS ✳ FRITOS ✳ *Pringles* ✳ *Funyuns* ✳ ANDY CAPP HOT FRIES ✳ BUGLES ✳ *Zonkers* ✳ *Kettle Chips* ✳ CRACKER JACKS ✳ COMBOS ✳ *Ruffles* ✳ *Pirate's Booty* ✳ CHEX MIX ✳ CHEESY POOFS ✳ WHITE CASTLE ✳ KFC ✳ *Taco Bell* ✳ *Jack in the Box* ✳ IN-N-OUT BURGER ✳ *Sonic* ✳ *Burger King* ✳ WENDY'S ✳ *McDonalds* ✳ *Arby's* ✳ POPEYE'S ✳ CHEBA HUT (West Coast chain) ✳ *Dairy Queen* ✳ *Denny's* ✳ FRIENDLY'S ✳ 7-11 ✳ *Your local convenience store* ✳ *Pizza Rolls* ✳ BAGEL BITES ✳ HOT POCKETS ✳ *Ho-Hos* ✳ *Yodels* ✳ RING DINGS ✳ DING DONGS ✳ *Devil Dogs* ✳ *Suzie Qs* ✳ TWINKIES ✳ TASTYKAKES ✳ *Moon Pies* ✳ *Fiber One Magic Brownies* ✳ GIRL SCOUT COOKIES ✳ PILLSBURY CINNAMON BUNS WITH WHITE FROSTING ✳ *Entenmann's entire oeuvre* ✳ *Little Debbie's entire catalog* ✳ GLAZED DONUTS ✳ CHOCOLATE FROSTED DONUTS ✳ *Apple-spice donuts* ✳ *Every other donut* ✳ CHEESECAKE ✳ BLACK FOREST CAKE ✳ *Strawberry shortcake* ✳ *Every other cake* ✳ LEMON MERINGUE PIE ✳ *Apple pie* ✳ SHOOFLY PIE ✳ EVERY OTHER PIE ✳ *Oreos* ✳ *Double Stuff Oreos* ✳ DOUBLE STUFF CHOCOLATE OREOS ✳ CHIPS AHOY ✳ *Nutter Butters* ✳ *Animal Crackers* ✳ POP TARTS ✳ PLAIN M&MS ✳ *Peanut M&Ms* ✳ SNICKERS ✳ *Reese's Peanut Butter Cups* ✳ *Reeses Pieces* ✳ RICE KRISPIES TREATS ✳ YORK PEPPERMINT PATTIES ✳ *Gummy bears* ✳ *Twix* ✳ MARS BAR ✳ CHARLESTON CHEW ✳ *Whatchamacallit* ✳ *$100,000 Bar* ✳ WONKA BAR ✳ CHUNKY ✳ *Honey Combs* ✳ *Cookie Crisp* ✳ FROSTED FLAKES ✳ PEANUT BUTTER CAP'N CRUNCH ✳ *Count Chocula* ✳ *Honey Bunches of Oats* ✳ SUPER SUGAR CRISPS ✳ RICE KRISPIES ✳ *Cocoa Pebbles* ✳ *Quisp* ✳ BEN AND JERRY'S CHERRY GARCIA ✳ BEN AND JERRY'S PHISH PHOOD ✳ *Ben and Jerry's Half Baked* ✳ *Everything on the ice cream truck* ✳ HOT DOGS ✳ HAMBURGERS ✳

Philly Cheesesteaks ✳ *Pizza* ✳ TACOS ✳ GYROS ✳ *Nachos* ✳ *Tater tots* ✳ JERKY (beef, turkey, buffalo, ostrich) ✳ PEANUTS ✳ *Saltines* ✳ *Spray cheese and crackers* ✳ PEANUT BUTTER CRACKERS ✳ FRIED CHICKEN ✳ *Chicken crispies* ✳ *Chicken tenders* ✳ CHICKEN RONDELETS ✳ CHICKEN WINGS ✳ *Pizza with barbecue chicken and red onions* ✳ *Pizza with pulled pork and applesauce* ✳ PIZZA WITH HOT DOGS AND BAKED BEANS ✳ PIZZA WITH WHATEVER'S-IN-THE-FRIDGE ✳ *Two pieces of toast with a hardboiled egg, syrup, and cinnamon* ✳ *Two pieces of toast with turkey, jalapeno cheese, Nutella, and gherkins* ✳ SIX PIECES OF TOAST WITH A TUB OF HUMMUS, CUCUMBER SLICES, BACON, AND PARMESAN CHUNKS ✳ *Crushed oil & vinegar potato chips with moose tracks ice cream and chocolate frosting between graham crackers* ✳ *Peanut butter and fried dill pickle sandwich* ✳ FROZEN CHERRIES IN MILK WITH CRUSHED CHOCOLATE GRAHAM CRACKERS ✳ TWO SALTINES, JERKY, SPRAY CHEESE, HOT MUSTARD, OLIVE SLICE ✳ *Peanut butter and chocolate chips on cinnamon raisin bread toast* ✳ *Microwave burritos with sour cream and hot-dog relish* ✳ SUB ROLL FILLED WITH PEANUT BUTTER AND JELLY, NUTELLA, BANANA CHUNKS, HONEY, AND CELERY ✳ PEANUT BUTTER AND CHOCOLATE CHIPS NUKED FOR 15 SECONDS, POURED OVER NEAPOLITAN ICE CREAM ✳ *Two cherry Pop Tarts filled with turkey, cheddar, bacon, toasted, with yogurt on top* ✳ *Popcorn, peanut, and cracker bowl with drizzled chocolate and mini marshmallows* ✳ PEANUT BUTTER AND JELLY WITH BACON ON SOURDOUGH TOAST ✳ MOZZARELLA STICKS WITH A SYRUP-MARINARA-HUMMUS-RELISH DIPPING SAUCE ✳ *Peanuts, barbecue potato chips, chocolate chips, dried cherries, and sour cream in a hot pita* ✳ *Froot Loops, strawberry yogurt, half and half, and frozen blueberries in a bowl* ✳ RASPBERRY TOASTER STREUDELS SPLATHERED WITH ALMOND BUTTER AND A GLASS OF COLD CHOCOLATE MILK ✳ M&Ms, PEANUT BUTTER, AND A SPOON ✳ *Delmonico steak, baked potato with sour cream and chives, and choice of veggie (cook all first, then hit the bong just after you plate the food)* ✳ *Garlic bread sandwich with hot roast beef, melted Parmesan, and coleslaw* ✳ PIEROGIES, BACON, SPRAY CHEESE, AND BAKED BEANS ON A WARM TORTILLA ✳ PORK ROLL AND CHEESE ON WHITE BREAD, LIGHTLY TOASTED ✳ *Corn dogs and chocolate milk* ✳ *Chinese food* ✳ MEXICAN FOOD ✳ ALL OTHER FOOD ✳ *5 Hour Energy* ✳ *Red Bull* ✳ JOLT COLA ✳ MOUNTAIN DEW ✳ *Mountain Dew Code Red* ✳ *Slurpees* ✳ ICEES ✳ SMOOTHIES ✳ MILKSHAKES ✳ *Chocolate milk* ✳ *Coffee* ✳ TEA ✳ BLUEBERRY ACAI WATER ✳ *Vitamin water* ✳ *Tap water* ✳ JUST DON'T DRINK THE BONG WATER!

SPOT THE
Differences

They say stoners can't concentrate, don't know what the hell is going on, are lazy, stupid, and smell. Well, it's time to prove them wrong with the old spot-the-differences game. Stare at the two pictures above to uncover the six differences between the picture on the left and the picture on the right.

1. _____

2. _____

3. _____

4. _____

5. _____

6. _____

Baby Names

Stoners are people, too. And they often get married, have sex, and procreate to give birth to little future stoners who will one day hold the mantle of stonerhood.

Whenever stoners have a bun in the oven, and they start thinking of what they're going to name Junior, there aren't a lot of different books and websites out there to separate all the hip naming ideas for their little bundles of joy, like these.

Boys Names

BERNIE	ICKY
BLAZE	JAY
BO	KEIF
BOB	KIFF
BRICK	LEIF
BUD	NICK
BUZZ	PHIL
CRISPY	PHILLY
DAG	PUFF DADDY
DOBIE	RIP
DUTCH	ROLLY
GAGE	SHAGGY
GRAM	SMOKEY
HENRY (THE "8TH")	SNOOP
	SPARKY
HERB	TRIP
HY	WEEDON

Girls Names

ASHLEY	MARE
BLUEBERRY	MARI
CHEEBA	MARLEY
CHERRY	MARY
CRYSTAL	MARY ANN
DUCHESS	MARY JANE
INDICA	MEG
INDO	M.J.
IRIE	SHIVA
JUANITA	YESCA
JUJA	
KAYA	
KAYBEE	
K.B.	
KATE BUSH	
LACEY	
LUCY	

SANTA CLAUS AND HIS OLD LADY

by Cheech & Chong

CHEECH: *(Playing piano)* "Ma-ma-ma-ma-cita, donde esta Santa Cleese... the vato wit' da bony knees... he comin' down da street wit' no choos on his feet... and he's going to..." No, no, that ain't it... "Mamamacita, donde esta Santa Claus... da guy wit da hair on his jaws... he's..." Nah. Hey, man, come over here, man. I need some help, man.

CHONG: Yeah, man. I can dig that. Like, uh, what are ya doin', man?

CHEECH: Aw, I'm trying to write a song about Santa Claus, man, but it's not comin' out...

CHONG: About who, man?

CHEECH: About Santa Claus, man. You know, Santa Claus, man?

CHONG: Oh, yeah, man. I played with those dudes, man.

CHEECH: What?

CHONG: Yeah, last year at the Fillmore, man. Me and the bass player sat in, man.

CHEECH: Oh, hey, man, you think Santa Claus is a group, huh? No, it's not a group, man.

CHONG: Wha'? They break up, man?

CHEECH: No, man. It's one guy, man. Y'know, he hada red suit on, man, with black patent leather choos... you know the guy, man.

CHONG: Oh, yeah... he's with Motown, ain't he? Yeah, I played with that dude, too, man. He's a good singer, man.

CHEECH: No, no, hold on, man. He's not with Motown, man.

CHONG: Well, then he's with Buddah, man.

CHEECH: No, aw, man, you don't know who Santa Claus is, man!

CHONG: Yeah, well, I'm not from here, man. Like, I'm from Pittsburgh, man. I don't know too many local dudes.

CHEECH: Ohhh, I see. Well, hey, man, sit back and relax and I'll tell you da story about Santa Claus, man. Listen...

(background music begins)

Once upon a time, about, hmmm, five years ago, there was this groovy dude and his name was Santa Claus, y'know? And he used to live over in the projects with his old lady and they had a pretty good thing together because his old lady was really fine and she could cook and all that stuff like that, y'know. Like, she made da best brownies in town, man! Oh, I could remember 'em now, man. I could eat one of 'em, man, wow...

CHONG: Wow, did you know these people, man?

CHEECH: Oh, yeah, man. They used to live next door to me, y'know... until they got kicked out, man.

CHONG: Wha'? They got kicked out of the projects, man?

CHEECH: Yeah, you know what happened, man? They used ta live with all these midgets, y'know, and da midgets used ta make a lotta noise, y'know, like pounding and hammering and pounding all night, man...

CHONG: Typical freaks, huh?

CHEECH: Oh, yeah, man, they were really freaks, man. As a matter of fact, they all moved up north together, y'know.

CHONG: Oh, they had to go get their head together, man?

CHEECH: Yeah, get their head together. And they started a commune, y'know. It was called the… uh…"Santa Claus and his Old Lady Commune"; it was a real famous one up there, man. And they used to sit around and groove all the time, y'know.

CHONG: Oh, yeah?

CHEECH: Yeah, a really good time, man.

CHONG: That sounds heavy.

CHEECH: Yeah, they eat da brownies, man, and they drink da tea, man… and what they did most of da time, though, was make a lotta goodies, y'know? And they had everything they needed; they only needed to come into town maybe once a year or something like that…

CHONG: To pick up the welfare check and the food stamps, right.

CHEECH: Yeah… No, no, what they did, man, is that, once a year, when they made all the goodies, y'know, they used ta put 'em in a beeg chopping bag and, then, they used ta take da chopping bag and give 'em to all the boys and girls all da way around da world, man!

CHONG: Hey, well, that's hip, man. That sounds real nice.

CHEECH: Oh, yeah, they were really nice people, man. And so much class, man… they had so much class, y'know. Like, even take da way they used ta deliver da toys, y'know. It's like, Santa Claus used ta have this really charp chort, man, y'know? It was lowered to da ground, had twice-pipes, candy-apple red and button top. Oooo, clean!

CHONG: Hey, that sounds like a hip snowmobile, man.

CHEECH: No, no, it wasn't a snowmobile; it was a sled, y'know. One of those big sleds, y'know? And he used ta have it pulled by some reindeers, y'know, like, reindeers?

CHONG: Some what, man?

CHEECH: Some reindeers, y'know. He used ta hook them onto da sled and then he used ta stand up inside da sled and hold on to da reins and then call out their names, like, "On Donner! On, Blitzen! On Chewy! On Tavo! C'mon, Becto!" And then, the reindeers used ta take off into da sky and fly across da sky, man!

CHONG: Wow, man! That's far out, man!

CHEECH: Yeah! And then, when they flied across da sky, they used ta come down to places like, oh, Chicago, L.A., Nueva York and Pacoima and all those places, y'know, and then land on top of people's roofs and then 'ol Santa Claus would make himself real small, y'know, like, a real small guy, and he'd come down da chimney and then he would give you all da stuff that he made, man. And… dig this, man… he did it all in one night, man!

CHONG: Hey, just a minute, man. Now, how'd he do that, man?

CHEECH: Oh, well, man, he took da freeway. How else, man?

CHONG: No, man. No, man, how'd he do all that other stuff, man? Like, how'd he make himself small, man. And, how'd he, like, how'd he get the reindeer off the ground, man?

CHEECH: Oh, well, man, he had some magic dust, man.

CHONG: Some magic dust?

CHEECH: Yeah, magic dust, y'know? He used ta give a little bit to da reindeer, a little bit to Santa Claus, a little bit more for Santa Claus, a little bit more...

CHONG And this would get the reindeer off, man?

CHEECH: Aw, got 'em off, man? Are you kidding, man? They flew all da way around da world, man!

CHONG: Hey, that's far out, man! Hey, how come I've never met this dude, man?

CHEECH: Oh, man, he doesn't do that bit anymore, man. It got too dangerous, man.

CHONG: Yeah, I can dig that, man, 'cause that's a dangerous bit, man!

CHEECH: Yeah, lemme tell ya, it sure was, man. Like just two years ago, man, he got stopped at the border, y'know, and they took him into another room and took off his clothes, man, and searched him and searched his bag of goodies, man... and then, when he was leaving, man, he was flying through the air and somebody took a chot at his reindeer, y'know.

CHONG: Aw, that's a drag, man.

CHEECH: Yeah, it really was, man. And then, man, he went down South, man, and they tried to cut off his hair and his beard, man. And all the time, he was getting stopped and pulled over and asked for his ID, man... just everywhere he went, he ran into too much recession, man.

CHONG: No, man, you mean he ran into too much repression, man.

CHEECH: Aw, "repression"..."recession"...man, it's all da same thing, man.

CHONG: Yeah, man. But, it's a drag, man, 'cause we could sure use a dude like that right now.

CHEECH: Oh, he still comes around, man.

CHONG: Oh, yeah?

CHEECH: Yeah, but he comes in disguises now...

CHONG: Aw, he went "underground".

CHEECH: Yeah, "underground", man.

CHONG: I can dig it.

CHEECH: Yeah. But you ought to see his disguise, man; nobody would ever know it was him, man.

CHONG: Oh, yeah?

CHEECH: Yeah. He's got a job in front of da department store, ringing this bell and playing this tambourine next to this black pot, y'know?

CHONG: Aw, I seen the dude, man!

CHEECH: Yeah! You know who I'm talking about, man!

CHONG: Yeah, man! I played with that cat last year, man!

CHEECH: Wha?

CHONG: Yeah, we played in front of a store, man! We made a lot of bread, man!

CHEECH: Aw, hey, wait a minute, man! Santa Claus is not a musician, man!

CHONG: I'm hip, man! That cat didn't know any tunes, man!

CHEECH: Oh, hey, wait a minute, man... no, he's not hip to that at all, man.

CHONG: No, I played with this dude, man.

CHEECH: Are you sure, man?

CHONG: Positive!

antici . . .

...*pation*

420-FRIENDLY?

Everyone knows the stereotypes used to describe stoners. Back in the '70s, they were all true. And today, well, they're still kinda true. It's harder to spot a stoner now because so many people from all walks of life are 420 fans. But from the looks to the clothes to the accessories to the way stoners talk and more, if at least a few of the major details below add up on a stranger, they're probably a stoner, and someone you can safely ask, "Wanna get high?"

The Looks

Bare feet, burnt fingertips from roaches, Doritos dust on fingers, dreadlocks, permasmile, red eyes, resin stains, sticky black substance on the bottom of their lighter, sunglasses at night, super-relaxed

The Clothes

Bandanas, bellbottoms, Birkenstocks, bright rasta colors (red, green, yellow), business casual clothes, Cheech and Chong baseball cap, classic-rock band tee shirt, Dead doodads, hippy poncho, tie-dyed clothes

Accessories

Disc-golf discs, DVD collection with every Cheech and Chong movie (plus *Half Baked*, *Harold and Kumar*, and *Pineapple Express*), extra empty baggies, flowers in hair, hacky sack, hemp baseball cap, hemp belt, hemp bracelet, hemp lantern, hemp scarf, hemp shoes, hemp wallet, lighter without cigarettes, Ozium in car, roach-clip jewelry, Visine, Volkswagon bus

Stoner Language

420, Are you cool?, Are you down?, bro, dank (used to describe anything as "good"), down, dude, far out, Have you seen my [fill in the blank], hip, Huh?, I've got the munchies, leisurely speech, man, rambling lofty insights, road trip!, What?

Et Cetera

Can't find car keys, can't find lighter, disappear at 4:20 every afternoon for fifteen minutes, frequent napping, great with fractions and metric conversions of ounces and grams, insatiable hunger, laughs at just about everything, lots of fast food wrappers in the car, out of cash, stole your lighter—again, sweet and slightly burnt aroma about them, there's a certain vibe about them, train of thought often gets derailed

Game On!

For stoners, marijuana is not a sport or hobby—it's a way of life. But it does make all kinds of games and sports and activities more fun and interesting to engage in and play, and a lot of stoners swear that they raise their game whenever they raise their spirits with some smoke. Don't believe it? Then consider this your starter stoner sports checklist and go get your game on at the highest level.

Adventure Racing

Archery

Australian Rules Football

Badminton

Bandy

Baseball

Basketball

Beach Volleyball

Bird Watching

Boating

Bobsledding

Bocce

Bodysurfing

Boomerang Throwing

Bowling

Broomball

Bubble Hockey

Bullfighting

Bungee Jumping

Buzbee

Camel Racing

Camping

Canoeing

Cave Diving

Cliff Diving

Cheerleading

Cricket

Curling

Cycling

Darts

Discus

Disc Golf

Dodgeball

Dog Sledding

Double Dutch

Elephant Polo

Falconry

Fencing

Field Hockey

Fishing

Foosball

Football

Frisbee

Frog Racing

Geocaching

Go Karting

Golf

Hacky Sack

Hammer Throw

Handball

Hang Gliding

Hide-and-Go-Seek

High Hurdles

Hiking

Hopscotch

Horseback Riding

Horseshoes

Hot-Air Ballooning

Hula Hooping

Hurling

Ice Fishing

Ice Hockey

Ice Skating

Javelin Toss

Jet Skiiing

Jogging

Kayaking

Kickball

Kite Flying

Knife Throwing

Lacrosse

Lawn Darts

Lawnmower Racing
Long Jump
Luge
Lumberjack Games
Marbles
Miniature Golf
Motocross
Mountain Biking
Mountaineering
Netball
Nude [Any Sport Here]
Off-Roading
Orienteering
Paddleball
Paintball
Pigeon Racing
Paragliding
Pinball
Pocketball
Pogo Stick
Polo
Pool
Power Boating
Quoits
Racquetball
Rafting
Rodeo
Roller Derby
Rounders
Rugby
Running

Sailing
Scrambling
Scuba Diving
Sheep Rustling
Shot Put
Shuffleboard
Shufflebowl
Skateboarding
Skiing
Skydiving
Sledding
Snowboarding
Snowmobiling
Snowshoeing
Soccer
Softball
Spearfishing
Squash
Stickball
Street Luge
Surfing
Swimming
Synchronized Swimming
Table Tennis
Tag
Tai Chi
Target Shooting
Tennis
Tetherball
Tobogganing
Tractor Pull

Trampolining
Tug of War
Turtle Racing
Ultimate
Unicycling
Wakeboarding
Wallyball
Water Ballet
Water Polo
Waterskiing
Whitewater
Rafting
Windsurfing
Wrestling
Working Out
Yoyo
Ziplining

DOODLE TIME

Take a toke, pick a pen, and doodle down. The theme for this page is . . .

Paraphernalia

FUN WITH ROLLING PAPERS

There's more than one way to have a good time with rolling papers. Flex your cannabis creativity muscle with some of these clever crafts that are fun for the whole family of stoners.

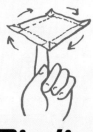

Rizzling

Rizzling is the amazing art of spinning rolling papers on your fingertips like magic as you walk around the room. Never thought you'd be dabbling in magic? Think again. Your friends will be comparing you to Doug Henning before you know it.

1. Get stoned.
2. Take a rolling paper and fold all sides in, about the width of the glue strip.
3. Unfold each of the four folds.
4. Pinch the four corners just to the width of the folds, to create what looks like a tray with pointy corners.
5. Prepare to amaze.
6. Put your index fingertip in the middle of the paper and start walking—it should start spinning.
7. If it doesn't work at first, try troubleshooting by: (a) loosening up the folds slightly; and if that doesn't work, (b) gently pinch the middle of the paper between your thumb and index finger, then releasing your thumb as you start walking.

Bracelet

Jewelry makes a great gift—whether you're giving it to a friend or to yourself. A rolling paper bracelet is an even greater gift considering all the potential you sacrificed in making it!

1. Do a bong hit.
2. Get the wrist size of the person you're making the bracelet for.

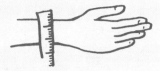

3. Lay out several rolling papers in a line, until they reach your desired length plus three extra inches.
4. With the glue strip facing up and at the top, fold the paper over, one-third of an inch at a time, from the bottom up until the last fold is flush with the top of the glue strip. Make sure the glue does not attach yet.

5. Repeat Step 4 with all of the papers.

6. Take two of the folded papers, one in each hand.

7. On the top-left corner of the right-hand paper, fold down one-eighth of an inch of the folded paper, exposing the corner of the glue strip.

8. Starting about a quarter inch from the left side, lick the glue strip on the left-hand paper, leaving the left side dry.

9. Lick the glue strip on the right-hand paper from the left to the right, stopping a half-inch from the right edge.

10. Slide the left edge of the right-hand paper between the last fold and the glue strip of the left-hand paper, and press it together. The glue strip from the left-hand paper will bind to the outside of the right-hand paper, and the glue from the right-hand paper will bind to the inside of the left-hand paper.

11. Repeat Steps 8-10 until all papers have been joined except for the first and last papers.

12. Wrap the paper string around the chosen wrist, and complete Steps 8-10 on the final two papers to complete the piece.

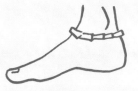

Anklet

Jewelry makes a great gift—whether you're giving it to a friend or to yourself. A rolling paper ~~bracelet~~ anklet is an even greater gift than a bracelet, considering the extra potential you sacrificed in making this longer piece!

1. Repeat all steps from the "Bracelet" instructions above, substituting "ankle" for "wrist" in Steps 2 and 12.

Necklace

Jewelry makes a great gift—whether you're giving it to a friend or to yourself. A rolling paper ~~bracelet anklet~~ necklace is an even greater gift than a cheapo bracelet or anklet, considering the sacrifice you made that will leave you with no more papers left to roll doobies!

1. Repeat all steps from the "Bracelet" instructions above, substituting "neck" for "wrist" in Steps 2 and 12.

Cat Toy

This is the easiest paper craft to accomplish; unfortunately, it takes up the largest amount of rolling papers. But your cat will absolutely love it*!

1. Get high.
2. Remove all sleeves from four or five packs of rolling papers
3. Scrunch them all up into a giant ball; as the ball grows, you'll have to lick the glue strip to get each new paper to stay on it
4. When all papers are on the ball, toss it to your cat.
5. Your cat will absolutely love it—*for several minutes—and then will be completely disinterested.

Paper Airplane

You can make a single-engine prop plane, or a jumbo jet—depends on how much paper you've got to spare. Personally, most of our papers are earmarked for other purposes, so we'll just focus on the classic one-seater.

1. Fire one up.
2. Use the largest-sized papers in your stoner kit—1.5s work pretty good.

3. Start with the paper folded in half on the original crease.
4. Fold the right corner of one side of the paper down to form a triangle, with the right side of the paper now flush with the bottom.

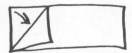

5. Flip the paper and repeat on the other side, even with the first fold.
6. Fold the triangle again to form another triangle, again making the fold flush with the bottom.

7. Flip the paper and repeat on the other side.
8. Turn off all personal electronics; your rolling-paper airplane is now ready for takeoff.

Mini Sculptures

Rolling papers are so thin and pliant, and yet so durable when handled with care, that they make an excellent media for sculpted art. And the thin glue strip allows the artist to create shapes that stay in place.

1. Smoke some weed.

2. Conceive the sculpture you want to make. This can come in a dream, a vision quest, or while riding the bus.

3. Sketch out your sculpture in two dimensions, then in three dimensions, on paper.

4. Draw a few extra sketches, just in case the finished work becomes famous—the extra sketches can be sold for some good money!

5. Get your papers in order, and start making art. At this point, you're pretty much on your own. But we're with you, spiritually.

Christmas Tree Garland

Make your holly-jolly Christmas even holly-jollier with this inventive string of garland.

I. Smoke a bone.

2. Lay out about fifty rolling papers in a line.

3. With the glue strip facing up and at the top, fold the paper over, one-third of an inch, from the bottom up. Repeat until the last fold is flush with the top of the glue strip. Make sure the glue does not attach yet.

4. Repeat Step 3 with all of the papers.

5. Take two of the folded papers, one in each hand.

6. On the top-left corner of the right-hand paper, fold down one-eighth of an inch of the folded paper, exposing the corner of the glue strip.

7. Lick the glue strip on the left-hand paper.

8. Lick the glue strip on the right-hand paper from the left to the right, stopping a half-inch from the right edge.

9. Slide the left edge of the right-hand paper between the bottom fold and the glue strip of the left-hand paper, and press the left-hand paper together along the glue strip. The glue strip from the left-hand paper will bind to itself and to the outside of the right-hand paper, and the glue from the right-hand paper will bind to the inside of the left-hand paper, creating a link.

10. Repeat Steps 7-9 until all papers have been

joined to create a long garland. You can string this classic-white garland on the tree now, or move on to Step 11.

II. Lay the garland on an old bedsheet and, doing two feet at a time, spray it with spray glue and immediately sprinkle it with sparkles.

12. After the glue and sparkles are dry, string your garland around and around the tree.

𝕱𝕚𝕟𝕚𝕤𝕙 𝕷𝕚𝕟𝕖

Haven't you always dreamed of running through one of those big finish-line paper strips at the end of a marathon foot race, with your arms up and a triumphant look on your face? Well, now you can make that dream a reality without ever leaving your living room.

1. Blaze.
2. Measure the opening of the doorway between your living room and kitchen (or some other doorway in your home).
3. Lay out several rolling papers in a line, until they reach your desired length plus ten extra inches.
4. Take two papers, one in each hand, folded along the pre-made horizontal fold out of the pack.
5. On the top-left corner of the right-hand paper, fold down one-eighth of an inch of the non-glue side of the paper, exposing the corner of the glue strip.
6. Starting about a quarter inch from the left side, lick the glue strip on the left-hand paper, leaving the left side dry.
7. Lick the glue strip on the right-hand paper from the left to the right, stopping a half-inch from the right edge.
8. Slide the left edge of the right-hand paper between the last fold and the glue strip of the left-hand paper, and press it together. The glue strip from the left-hand paper will bind to the outside of the right-hand paper, and the glue from the right-hand paper will bind to the inside of the left-hand paper.
9. Repeat Steps 6-8 until all papers have been joined except for the first and last papers.
10. Lick the last bit of glue on the last left-hand link and press it against the door frame on one side, then lick the last bit of glue on the last right-hand link and press it against the door frame on the other side.
11. Prepare for glory.

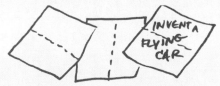

𝕹𝕠𝕥𝕖𝕤 𝕥𝕠 𝕾𝕖𝕝𝕗

We don't know who invented sticky notes, but our guess it was a stoner, because look at it. It's a thicker rolling paper with a less-sticky glue strip. Do it.

1. Bake.
2. Try to remember what it was that you wanted to remember.
3. Take out a rolling paper and write a note-to-self on the side opposite the glue strip.
4. Lick the glue strip and stick it to a wall where you will be sure to see it.
5. Procrastinate; you can get to that note-to-self later.

POT PLAYLIST

Here's a stoner-song starter playlist for stoners and their stoner friends. We could have, but didn't, include every song ever recorded by Bob Marley and Snoop Dogg—but certainly a few of theirs are here. And if we forgot any of your favorites, it's only because we forgot.

"100 Weight of Collie Weed" by Sublime

"420" by the Kottonmouth Kings

"Acid Raindrops" by People Under the Stairs

"Addicted" by Amy Winehouse

"African Herbsman" by Bob Marley and the Wailers

"Are You In?" by Incubus

"Bad Weed Blues" by Bone Thugs N Harmony

"Because I Got High" by Afroman

"Big Spliff" by Murphy's Law

"Blazin'" by Nicki Minaj

"Blueberry Yum Yum" by Ludacris featuring Sleepy Brown

"Blunt to My Lips" by Project Pat

"Bong Hits for Breakfast" by Staind

"Born in East LA" by Cheech and Chong

"Brown Sugar" by D'Angelo

"Burn One Down" by Ben Harper

"Cali Dro" by Birdman and Lil Wayne

"Can I Get a Hit?" by Cypress Hill

"Champagne and Reefer" by Muddy Waters

"Cheeba Cheeba" by Tone-Loc

"City Hall" by Tenacious D

"Come Downstairs and Say Hello" by Guster

"Coming into Los Angeles" by Arlo Guthrie

"Copperhead Road" by Steve Earle

"Crumblin' Erb" by Outkast

"The Crunge" by Led Zeppelin

"A Day in the Life" by the Beatles

"Day 'n' Nite" by Kid Cudi

"Don't Bogart Me" by Fraternity of Man

"Don't Bogart That Joint" by Country Joe and the Fish

"Don't Step On the Grass, Sam" by Steppenwolf

FROM LEFT: *Crosby, Stills and Nash • Ray Charles • Bob Dylan • Muse • Cypress Hill*

"**Doobie Ashtray**" *by Devin the Dude*

"**Drugs**" *by Lil Kim*

"**Easy Skankin'**" *by Bob Marley*

"**Everybody Must Get Stoned**" *by Cyprus Hill*

"**Everybody's Smoking Cheeba**" *by The Donnas*

"**Feelin' It**" *by Jay-Z*

"**Flying High Again**" *by Ozzy Osbourne*

"**Framed**" *by Cheech and Chong*

"**Front Porch**" *by Twista*

"**Fuckin' Wit' Dank**" *by Ant Banks*

"**Gangsta Lean**" *by Clipse*

"**Ganja Bus**" *by Cyprus Hill and Damian Marley*

"**Ganja of Love**" *by Jefferson Starship*

"**Get High Tonight**" *by Busta Rhymes*

"**Gin and Juice**" *by Snoop Dogg*

"**Good Times (I Get High)**" *by Styles P*

"**Gospel Weed Song**" *by Bizarre*

"**Got to Get You Into My Life**" *by the Beatles*

"**Green Day**" *by Green Day*

"**Hail the Leaf**" *by Down*

"**Hashpipe**" *by Weezer*

"**High All the Time**" *by 50 Cent*

"**High Head Blues**" *by the Black Crowes*

"**High Time**" *by the Grateful Dead*

"**Hits from the Bong**" *by Cypress Hill*

"**Hold It Now, Hit It**" *by the Beastie Boys*

"**Homegrown**" *by Neil Young*

"**Hotel California**" *by the Eagles*

"**How High**" *by Method Man and Redman*

"**How to Roll a Blunt**" *by Redman*

"**Hydroponic**" *by 311*

"**I Can't Wake Up**" *by KRS-One*

"**If You're a Viper**" *by Leroy "Stuff" Smith*

"**I Get High**" *by Lloyd Banks feat. 50 Cent and Snoop Dogg*

"**I Get High**" *by Styles P*

"**I Get Lifted**" *by KC and the Sunshine Band*

"**I Got 5 On It**" *by The Luniz*

"**I Got Stoned and I Missed It**" *by Shel Silverstein*

"**I Like Marijuana**" *by David Peel and the 360s*

"**I Love College**" *by Asher Roth*

"**I Smoke Weed**" *by Eminem feat. Snoop Dogg*

"**I Wanna Get High**" *by Cypress Hill*

"**I'm Awesome**" *by Spose*

"**In the Cut**" *by Wiz Khalifa*

"**Indo Smoke**" *by Mister Grimm*

"**Insane in the Brain**" *by Cyprus Hill*

"**The Joker**" *by Steve Miller Band*

"**Kaya**" *by Bob Marley and the Wailers*

"**Kronic**" *by Lil' Kim*

"**La Cucaracha**" *by Traditional Mexican/Spanish Folk Song*

"**Last Dance with Mary Jane**" *by Tom Petty*

"**Legalize It**" *by Peter Tosh*

"**Let's Get High**" *by Dr. Dre feat. Hittman, Kurupt & Ms. Roq*

"**Let's Get Stoned**" *by Sublime*

"**Let's Go Get Stoned**" *by Ray Charles*

"**(Let's Go) Smoke Some Pot**" *by Dash Rip Rock*

"**Light Up or Leave Me Alone**" *by Traffic*

"**Marijuana**" *by Kid Cudi*

"**Marijuana**" *by Phish*

"**Marijuana Mix**" *by Eminem*

"**Marrakesh Express**" *by Crosby, Stills & Nash*

"**Martha**" *by Jefferson Airplane*

"Mary Jane" by Rick James

"Mexican Americans" by Cheech and Chong

"Misty Mountain Hop" by Led Zeppelin

"Moist Vagina" by Nirvana

"Mota" by the Offspring

"Muggles" by Louis Armstrong

"Natural Mystic" by Bob Marley

"One Draw" by Rita Marley

"One Toke Over the Line" by Brewer and Shipley

"The Next Episode" by Dr. Dre featuring Snoop Dogg and Nate Dogg

"The No No Song" by Ringo Starr

"Pack the Pipe" by The Pharcyde

"Panama Red" by New Riders of the Purple Sage

"A Passage to Bangkok" by Rush

"Pass That Dutch" by Missy Elliott

"Pass the Dutchie" by Musical Youth

"Pass the Kouchie" by Mighty Diamonds

"Peaches n Erb" by Society of Soul

"Peer Pressure" by De La Soul

"Pencil Thin Mustache" by Jimmy Buffet

"Police in Helicopter" by John Holt

"Puff the Magic Dragon" by Peter, Paul, and Mary

"Purple Haze" by Jimi Hendrix

"The Pusher" by Steppenwolf

"Pusher Man" by Curtis Mayfield

"Rainy Day Women #12 and 35" by Bob Dylan

"Reefer Man" by Cab Calloway

"The Reefer Song" by Fats Waller

"Rest of My Life" by Kottonmouth Kings

"Riding High" by Bob Marley and The Wailers

"Roll Another Number (For the Road)" by Neil Young

"Roll Up" by Wiz Khalifa

"Seeds & Stems (Again)" by Commander Cody and His Lost Planet Airmen

"Sinsemilla" by Black Uhuru

"Smoke On" by ESG

"Smoke Two Joints" by Sublime

"Smokin' Cheeba Cheeba" by George Benson

"Smokin'" by Nas

"Something about Mary" by Wyclef Jean

"Still Blazing" by Wiz Khalifa

"Stoned Is the Way of the Walk" by Cypress Hill

"Sugar Magnolia" by the Grateful Dead

"Sunday Morning Coming Down" by Johnny Cash

"Sweet Leaf" by Black Sabbath

"Take A Toke" by C+C Music Factory

"Take Two and Pass" by Gang Starr

"Tical" by Method Mann

"Up In Smoke" by Cheech and Chong

"Vaporize" by Broken Bells

"We Be Burnin'" by Sean Paul

"Weed Song" by Bone Thugs-N-Harmony

"Weed Got Me Crazy" Tupac

"Weed With Willie" by Toby Keith

"What If God Smoked Cannibas" by Bob Rivers

"Where's Da Bud?" by Three Six Mafia

"You Don't Know How It Feels" by Tom Petty

"Yes Please" by Muse

GAMES STONERS PLAY

Stoners like to have a good time, all the time. Even though a good time can be had by stoners anytime by just sitting there, sometimes it's fun to energize the room with one of these stoner games.

STARING CONTEST

Get a friend. Get two joints or a party bong. Both take a hit at the same time. Stare into each other's eyes, and whoever laughs or exhales first, loses, and has to pay up on a pre-agreed penalty.

NAME GAME

A fun way to pass the time while you pass the joint among friends. First, name a topic—Bands and Musicians. The first person takes a hit and passes to the left while saying any band or musician name— Bob Marley. The second person has ten seconds to think of another band name that begins with the last letter of Marley—"Yardbirds". If nothing comes to mind, they have to pass the joint without taking a hit. Wah-wah-waaah. You can keep doing musicians, or change the topic every time around the circle—movies, TV shows, cars, places, strains of weed, snack foods, etc.

DON'T SAY WHAT

The object of the game is to see how long you and your friends can go without saying the word, what.

Whenever someone says what, someone else has to say "You said what," and the offender has to pack a bowl.

Once everyone in the room agrees to play, the game is on.

The strategy is to try to get someone to say what however you can—mumble something; talk in a foreign language; say a sentence that makes no sense; ask if someone has ever seen a "henway."

("Hey man, have you ever seen a henway?" "What's a henway?" "You said what—pack a bowl! And by the way, a hen weighs about three pounds.")

The game ends when everyone forgets you're still playing, but can be resumed by any of the players for up to 48 hours whenever someone says what.

TAXI

Get your friends to sit in a circle. Each person takes a hit, passes it left, and must hold in their hit until the joint comes back to them. If you laugh or exhale or otherwise lose your smoke, you miss your next turn! Amp up the game by adding to the number of hits each player must take/hold before exhaling.

ONE WORD PASS

This is the game where you make up a story one word at a time as the doobie burns down. The first person takes a toke, says a word, and passes left. The second person takes a toke and says a second word to follow the first, then passes left. Each person has to keep the sentence going with the next word, and the more outrageous the details, the better. Continue around the circle until the joint becomes too small to hit—or until everyone is laughing too hard to keep going.

CONVENIENCE STORE

Go to a convenience store with friends and see who can get in and out without laughing out loud. First one to crack up buys the snacks.

TRUE/FALSE

You hand the joint to the person to your left. As they're taking a hit, you make a statement to them, ending with "true or false?" They have to answer during their exhale—"true" or "false" and then make a statement to the next person. Go clockwise until everyone gets a turn, and go again if you're having fun.

POST OFFICE

It's the classic parlor game where you say something to one person, and they pass it down the line to the next person, and so on, until it gets to the last person in line who repeats it back, out loud—usually all wrong. This is the game stoners sometimes play without knowing they're playing it.

Great Quotations

A lot of highly evolved people have proudly used cannabis for a long time—and many others who may not use it are at least wise and compassionate enough to stand up for an end to prohibition—from America's founding fathers to the leader of the evangelical church. That's right, George Washington grew it, and Pat Robertson wants Uncle Sam to legalize it! Read these inspiring words of wisdom, and use these quotes when making your case to the unenlightened.

"We shall, by and by, want a world of hemp more for our own consumption."

—JOHN ADAMS

"I was a heavy drinker, but the alcohol affected my heart rather than my liver. So I stopped. I smoke grass now. I say that to everybody, because marijuana should be legalized. It's ridiculous that it isn't. If at the end of the day I feel like smoking a joint, I do it. It changes the perception of what I've been through all day."
—ROBERT ALTMAN

"I enjoy smoking cannabis and see no harm in it." —JENNIFER ANISTON

"It really puzzles me to see marijuana connected with narcotics . . . dope and all that crap. It's a thousand times better than whiskey—it's an assistant, a friend."

—LOUIS ARMSTRONG

"You bet I did [inhale marijuana]—and I enjoyed it." —MAYOR MICHAEL BLOOMBERG

"We were high all the time, sneaking off to the walk-in refrigerator at every opportunity to 'conceptualize.' Hardly a decision was made without drugs."

—ANTHONY BOURDAIN

"It was absolutely about pot. . . . We were trying to be the Cheech and Chong of punk rock."

—BILLIE JOE ARMSTRONG, ON THE MEANING OF "GREEN DAY"

"By any of the major criteria of harm—mortality, morbidity, toxicity, addictiveness and relationship with crime—cannabis is less harmful than any of the other major illicit drugs, or than alcohol or tobacco."

—BRITISH POLICE FOUNDATION

"There is only one thing wrong with drug law enforcement, just one—it doesn't work. And when I tell you this I want you to believe me because I have done it."

—U.S. FEDERAL JUDGE VOLNEY BROWN JR.

"Marijuana is rejected all over the world. Damned. In England heroin is alright for outpatients, but marijuana? They'll put your ass in jail. I wonder why that is? The only reason could be: To Serve the Devil—Pleasure! Pleasure, which is a dirty word in Christian culture."
—LENNY BRUCE

"Narcotics police are an enormous, corrupt international bureaucracy . . . and now fund a coterie of researchers who provide them with 'scientific support' . . . fanatics who distort the legitimate research of others. . . . The anti-marijuana campaign is a cancerous tissue of lies, undermining law enforcement, aggravating the drug problem, depriving the sick of needed help, and suckering well-intentioned conservatives and countless frightened parents."

—WILLIAM F. BUCKLEY

"I was arrested for possession and cultivation of marijuana in the early '70s, and it was thrown out. The judge asked me how I felt about it, and I said, 'I understand the law, and I want you to know I'll pay the fine, but I cannot guarantee I will not break this law again.' He really chewed me out for that."

—GEORGE CARLIN

"Penalties against possession of a drug should not be more damaging to an individual than the use of the drug itself; and where they are, they should be changed. Nowhere is this more clear than in the laws against possession of marijuana in private for personal use. . . . Therefore, I support legislation amending Federal law to eliminate all Federal criminal penalties for the possession of up to one ounce of marijuana."

—JIMMY CARTER

"I don't do drugs . . . just weed."

—DAVE CHAPELLE

"It's not even the drugs that will kill you man. What really kills you is looking for drugs."

—TOMMY CHONG

"When you return to this mundane sphere from your visionary world, you would seem to leave a Neapolitan spring for a Lapland winter—to quit paradise for earth—heaven for hell! Taste the hashish, guest of mine—taste the hashish!"

—ALEXANDER DUMAS

"I think America's view on weed is ridiculous. I mean, are you kidding me? If everyone smoked weed, the world would be a better place."

—KIRSTEN DUNST

"The prestige of government has undoubtedly been lowered considerably by the prohibition law. For nothing is more destructive of respect for the government and the law of the land than passing laws which cannot be enforced. It is an open secret that the dangerous increase of crime in this country is closely connected with this."

—ALBERT EINSTEIN

"I say legalize drugs because I want to see less drug abuse, not more. And I say legalize drugs because I want to see the criminals put out of business." —EDWARD ELLISON, SCOTLAND YARD

"Free Marc." —EVERYONE

"Why use up the forests which were centuries in the making and the mines which required ages to lay down, if we can get the equivalent of forest and mineral products in the annual growth of the hemp fields?" —HENRY FORD

"If you look at the drug war from a purely economic point of view, the role of the government is to protect the drug cartel."

—MILTON FRIEDMAN

"I smoke a lot of pot when I write music."

—LADY GAGA

"Pot." —ZACH GALIFIANAKIS

"Marijuana is a useful catalyst for specific optical and aural aesthetic perceptions. I apprehended the structure of certain pieces of jazz and classical music in a new manner under the influence of marijuana, and these apprehensions have remained valid in years of normal consciousness."

—ALLEN GINSBERG

> ## "Smoking helped put me in touch with the realm of the senses."
> —HUGH HEFNER

"If John Lennon is deported, I'm leaving too . . . with my musicians . . . and my marijuana."
—ART GARFUNKEL

"We're here to do something historic. Around the issue of social justice, I go to a great number of incarceration houses where I see men and women incarcerated for a small amount of marijuana. Their lives are being changed and impacted, it's been catastrophic."
—DANNY GLOVER

"I give you every seed-bearing plant on the face of the whole earth and every tree that has fruit with seed in it."
—GOD

"Marijuana doesn't make me do anything that I wouldn't be capable of doing otherwise. I find it far more pleasant than drinking, less messy and more private. I never had the patience to sit in a bar and drink. Having a joint is far more economical and more immediate. I'm able to switch into certain inner places with marijuana."
—ELLIOT GOULD

"It is beyond my comprehension that any humane person would withhold such a beneficial substance [marijuana] from people in such great need simply because others use it for different purposes."
—STEPHEN JAY GOULD

"Since you [U.S. 'Drug Czar' Barry McCaffrey] control a federal budget that has just been increased from $17.8 billion last year to $19.2 billion this year, is asking people like you if we should continue with our nation's current drug policy like a person asking a barber if one needs a haircut?"
—JUDGE JAMES P. GRAY, ORANGE COUNTY, CA

"Many medical marijuana patients are too sick to grow their own. . . . It is time to show compassion and common sense. The people getting hurt in all of this are patients. They have a prescription from a doctor but they can't get it filled."
—WASHINGTON GOVERNOR CHRISTINE GREGOIRE

"Marijuana is one of the least-toxic substances in the whole pharmacopoeia."
—PROFESSOR LESTOR GRINSPOON, HARVARD MED SCHOOL

"I've seen it printed that I'm a marijuana activist, and I understand that, but it's really just something I enjoy."
—WOODY HARRELSON, MARIJUANA ACTIVIST

"If you substitute marijuana for tobacco and alcohol, you'll add eight to twenty-four years to your life." —JACK HERER

"Why is pot against the law? It wouldn't be because anyone can grow it, and therefore you can't make a profit off it, would it?"

—BILL HICKS

"Complete prohibition of all chemical mind changers can be decreed, but cannot be enforced, and tends to create more evils than it cures." —ALDOUS HUXLEY

"Legalize cannabis? Why? As far as I'm concerned, it's already fucking legal, so what's the point?" —JAMIROQUAI

"Hemp is of first necessity to the wealth and protection of the country."

—THOMAS JEFFERSON

"Western governments . . . will lose the war against dealers unless efforts are switched to prevention and therapy. . . . All penalties for drug users should be dropped. . . . Making drug abuse a crime is useless and even dangerous. . . . Every year we seize more and more drugs and arrest more and more dealers but at the same time the quantity available in our countries still increases. . . . Police are losing the drug battle worldwide."

—RAYMOND KENDALL,
SECRETARY GENERAL OF INTERPOL

"To be just without being mad (and the madder you get the madder you get), to be peaceful without being stupid, to be interested without being compulsive, to be happy without being hysterical . . . smoke grass." —KEN KESEY

"In any civilized society, it is every citizen's responsibility to obey just laws. But at the same time, it is every citizen's responsibility to disobey unjust laws."

—MARTIN LUTHER KING JR.

"I think that marijuana should not only be legal, I think it should be a cottage industry. It would be wonderful for the state of Maine. There's some pretty good homegrown dope. I'm sure it would be even better if you could grow it with fertilizers and have greenhouses."

—STEPHEN KING

"Whatever I'm already doing becomes enhanced when I smoke pot." —CHRISSIE HYNDE

"I owe a lot of the good ideas I've ever had in my life to pot." —BILL MAHER

"It gets you high, it makes you laugh, it does not produce a hangover. Unlike alcohol, it does not result in bar fights or wife beating. So, why is this innocuous plant illegal? Is it a gateway drug? No, that would be alcohol, which is so heavily advertised in this country. My only conclusion as to why it is illegal, is that Corporate America, which owns Congress, would rather sell you Paxil, Zoloft, Xanax and other addictive drugs, than allow you to grow a plant in your home without some of the profits going into their coffers." —ANDREW LAHDE

"They've outlawed the number-one vegetable on the planet." —DR. TIMOTHY LEARY

"Smoking's a way to let you down slowly from a ballgame. It also makes you use less of the resources around. It makes people better in the way they act towards society. Everybody's nicer. It's hard to be mean when you're stoned." —BILL "SPACEMAN" LEE

"Prohibition . . . goes beyond the bounds of reason in that it attempts to control a man's appetite by legislation and makes a crime out of things that are not crimes. A prohibition law strikes a blow at the very principles upon which our government was founded." —ABRAHAM LINCOLN

"I think that most American people want to be law abiding, and given an opportunity to purchase marijuana in a regulated scheme, and not violate the law, that they would choose that as an option. Further if you are selling it under a regulated scheme, you have quality control and you know exactly what the substance is that is being sold and . . . at a regulated point-of-sale, that you can impose warning labels like you do for the sale of alcohol or tobacco." —CHARLES MANDIGO, FORMER HEAD OF THE FBI IN SEATTLE

"It's a democratic process, and nobody is forcing marijuana down anybody's throat, and nobody is forcing beer down anybody's throat. They can go and have a beer or martini, so I should be able to smoke a joint if I want one." —CHEECH MARIN

"I used to smoke marijuana. But I'll tell you something: I would only smoke it in the late evening. Oh, occasionally the early evening, but usually the late evening—or the mid-evening. Just the early evening, mid-evening, and late evening. Occasionally, early afternoon, early mid-afternoon, or perhaps the late-mid-afternoon. Oh, sometimes the early-mid-late-early morning. . . . But never at dusk." —STEVE MARTIN

"When you smoke the herb, it reveals you to yourself."

—BOB MARLEY

"I think the 'Just say no' mentality is so crazed. I saw a thing in a women's magazine the other day. 'He smokes cannabis, what am I to do? He laughs it off when I try to tell him, he says it's not really harmful. . . .' Of course you're half hoping the advice will be, 'Well, you know it's not that harmful; if you love him, if you talk to him about it, tell him maybe he should keep it in the garden shed or something,' you know, a reasonable point of view. But of course it was, 'No, no, all drugs are bad. Librium's good, Valium's good. But cannabis, ooooh!' I hate that unreasoned attitude."   —PAUL McCARTNEY

"If the words 'life, liberty and the pursuit of happiness' don't include the right to experiment with your own consciousness, then the Declaration of Independence isn't worth the hemp it was written on."   —TERENCE McKENNA

"Marijuana is the finest anti-nausea medication known to science."   —PETER McWILLIAMS

"The only effect that I ever noticed from smoking marijuana was a sort of mild sedative, a release of tension when I was overworking. It never made me boisterous or quarrelsome. If anything, it calmed me and reduced my activity."

—ROBERT MITCHUM

"As an artist, there's a sweet jump-starting quality to it [marijuana] for me. I've often felt telepathic and receptive to inexplicable messages my whole life. I can stave those off when I'm not high. When I'm high—well, they come in and there's less of a veil, so to speak. So if ever I need some clarity . . . or a quantum leap in terms of writing something, it's a quick way for me to get to it."   —ALANIS MORISSETTE

"Marihuana's relative potential for harm to the vast majority of individual users and its actual impact on society does not justify a social policy designed to seek out and firmly punish those who use it. This judgment is based on prevalent use patterns, on behavior exhibited by the vast majority of users and on our interpretations of existing medical and scientific data. This position also is consistent with the estimate by law enforcement personnel that the elimination of use is unattainable."

—NATIONAL COMMISSION ON
MARIHUANA AND DRUG ABUSE, 1972

"I think people need to be educated to the fact that marijuana is not a drug. Marijuana is an herb and a flower. God put it here. If He put it here and He wants it to grow, what gives the government the right to say that God is wrong?"

—WILLIE NELSON

"Is marijuana addictive? Yes, in the sense that most of the really pleasant things in life are worth endlessly repeating." —RICHARD NEVILLE

"If one seeks relief from unbearable pressure, one is to eat hashish." —FRIEDRICH NIETZSCHE

"When I was a kid I inhaled [marijuana] frequently. That was the point." —BARACK OBAMA

"I would absolutely never use the federal government to enforce the law against anybody using marijuana." —RON PAUL

"Marijuana should definitely be legalized. I think we should let everyone smoke it without fear of being thrown in jail. It's the greatest drug in the world!" —MICHELLE PHILLIPS

"When pure and administered carefully, cannabis is one of the most useful medicines we possess." —SIR RUSSELL REYNOLDS, PHYSICIAN TO QUEEN VICTORIA

"I really believe we should treat marijuana the way we treat beverage alcohol. I've never used marijuana and I don't intend to, but it's just one of those things that I think: this war on drugs just hasn't succeeded." —PAT ROBERTSON

"I like to smoke pot and work out. To the ill-informed or the uninitiated in the magical ways of the sacred plant, this can seem like a very contradictory practice. In fact though, that notion could not be further from the truth." —JOE ROGAN

"When I first came to L.A., I got caught smoking weed on a beach in Malibu and had to go to court. It was the craziest thing ever. I was thinking, 'We're in Los Angeles. There are probably four hundred people getting murdered at this second, and these two cops are taking an hour to write up my court summons for smoking a joint on the beach.' That just seemed so fucking ridiculous to me." —SETH ROGAN

"The illegality of cannabis is outrageous, an impediment to full utilization of a drug which helps produce the serenity and insight, sensitivity and fellowship so desperately needed in this increasingly mad and dangerous world." —CARL SAGAN

"The lesson has already been learned with alcohol prohibition. We tried to engineer an alcohol-free society and ended up with huge criminal enterprises, government corruption, children lured into organized crime and random violence that took the lives of countless innocent people." —BALTIMORE MAYOR KURT SCHMOKE

"I've never had a problem with drugs. I've had a problem with the police."

—KEITH RICHARDS

"That is not a drug. That is a leaf."

—ARNOLD SCHWARZENEGGER

"I know you're supposed to tell kids not to do drugs, but, kids, do it! Do weed! Don't do the other stuff, but weed is good. . . ."

—KEVIN SMITH

"The War on Drugs has failed, but it's worse than that. It is actively harming our society. Violent crime is thriving in the shadows to which the drug trade has been consigned. People who genuinely need help can't get it. Neither can people who need medical marijuana to treat terrible diseases. We are spending billions, filling up our prisons with non-violent offenders and sacrificing our liberties." —STING

"Vietnamese grass is one of the most powerful, transforming herbs in the world. When I got high on that stuff, listening to Smokey, that's when I began to understand that life is sacred, that life has great vibrancy, which, in my case, was a perception I couldn't get out of."

—OLIVER STONE

"For my part, I find the attempt to ban any naturally growing plant to be an attack on reality, and a denial of some of the most basic freedoms. I guess that's why today's GOP is so in favor of it."

—ANDREW SULLIVAN

"Finally, the fundamental flaw, which will ultimately destroy this prohibition as it did the last one, is that criminal sanctions cannot, and should not attempt to, prohibit personal conduct which does no harm to others."

—JUDGE ROBERT SWEET, NEW YORK

"I'm a huge pothead, and a big fan of legalization, so I'm happy to talk about it."

—ROB THOMAS

"I have always loved marijuana. It has been a source of joy and comfort to me for many years. And I still think of it as a basic staple of life, along with beer and ice and grapefruits—and millions of Americans agree with me."

—HUNTER S. THOMPSON

"I'm for legalizing marijuana. Why pick on those drugs? Valium is legal. You just go to a doctor and get it and overdose on it—what's the difference? Prozac, all that stuff. So why not marijuana? Who cares? It's something that grows out of the ground—why not? Go smoke a head of cabbage. I don't care what you smoke." —HOWARD STERN

"Make the most of the Indian hemp seed, and sow it everywhere!"

—GEORGE WASHINGTON

"Estimates of Mexican cartel profits from marijuana sales to the U.S. vary from $2 billion to $20 billion annually. And recent studies suggest that the Colorado and Washington pot laws could dent cartel profits by up to 30% given the probable emergence of cheaper, U.S.-produced marijuana." —TIME

"Tylenol is legal, but if you take thirteen of those motherfuckers it'll be your last headache. As long as you live you ain't never heard of a motherfucker overdose on marijuana. You might think he's dead; he ain't dead! He's gonna wake up in thirty minutes hungry enough to eat up everything in your house. That's the side effects: happy, hungry and sleepy." —KATT WILLIAMS

"Everything is better when you're high." —WIZ KHALIFA

"Estimates suggest that from twenty to fifty million Americans routinely, albeit illegally, smoke marijuana without the benefit of direct medical supervision. Yet, despite this long history of use and the extraordinarily high numbers of social smokers, there are simply no credible reports to suggest that consuming marijuana has caused a single death. By contrast, aspirin, a commonly used, over-the-counter medicine, causes hundreds of deaths each year." —DEA JUDGE FRANCIS L. YOUNG

"One of the many things I've learned about weed is that not only does it make you feel good, and spark creativity from time to time, but it's also one of those things that bring people together no matter what culture, ethnicity, or social class." —B REAL

ASPIRATION

Size matters.

Movie Queue

You don't have to smoke alone if you watch one of these movies that all have at least one good pot scene, or ten.

24-Hour Party People
30 Minutes or Less
The 40-Year-Old Virgin
The 420 Movie
Accepted
The Acid House
Across the Universe
Adam and Paul
Adulthood
Adventureland
After Hours
Ali G Indahouse

Almost Famous
Alpha Dog
American Beauty
American Psycho
Amsterdam
Animal Kingdom
Annie Hall
Apocalypse Now
Assassin of Youth
Attack the Block
Awaydays
Bad Lieutenant

Bad Teacher
Bang Boom Bang
The Basketball Diaries
The Beach
Beerfest
Bickford Schmeckler's Cool Ideas
Bill & Ted's Excellent Adventure
Bio-Dome
The Big Chill
The Big Lebowski

Black Sheep

Blazing Saddles

Bodies, Rest & Motion

Bong of the Dead

Bongwater

Boogie Nights

Borderland

Born in East L.A.

The Breakfast Club

Brewster McCloud

Bug

A Bug and a Bag of Weed

Bully

Caddyshack

Cheech and Chong's Animated Movie

Cheech and Chong The Corsican Brothers

Cheech and Chong Get Out of My Room

Cheech and Chong's Hey Watch This

Cheech and Chong's Next Movie

Cheech and Chong's Nice Dreams

Cheech and Chong Things Are Tough All Over

Cheech and Chong Still Smokin'

Cheech and Chong's Up In Smoke

City of God

Clerks

Clueless

Club Paradise

The Cool and the Crazy

Dazed and Confused

Death at a Funeral

Detroit Rock City

Dick

District 13

Don't Be a Menace to South Central While Drinking Your Juice in the Hood

Don't Tell Mom the Babysitter's Dead

The Doors

Dude, Where's My Car?

Due Date

Easy Rider

Ed

Eternal Sunshine of the Spotless Mind

EuroTrip

Everything's Gone Green

Evil Bong

Evil Bong 2: King Bong

Evil Weed

Eyes Wide Shut

Far Out Man

Fast Times at Ridgemont High

Fear and Loathing in Las Vegas

Ferris Bueller's Day Off

Forrest Gump

Freak Talks about Sex

Friday

Friday After Next

Friends with Money

Fritz the Cat

Garden State

Get Out of My Room

Get Him to the Greek

Get Rich or Die Tryin'

Girl, Interrupted

The Girl Next Door

Go

The Gods Must Be Crazy

The Good Girl

Grandma's Boy

Grass

Grindhouse

Grounded for Life

Growing Op

I Heart Huckabees

Half Baked

Harold & Kumar: A Very Harold & Kumar Christmas

Harold & Kumar Escape from Guantanamo Bay

Harold & Kumar Go to White Castle

Harsh Times

Head

High Society: A Pot Boiler

History of the World: Part 1

A Home at the End of the World

Homegrown

Hot Fuzz

Hot Rod

Hot Tub Time Machine

How High

How Weed Won the West

Humboldt County

Hustle & Flow

Idle Hands

Igby Goes Down

In the Weeds

It Came from Hollywood

It's Complicated

Jackie Brown

Jay and Silent Bob Strike Back

Joe Dirt

Kick Ass

Kids

Killer Bud

Knocked Up

Kush

Leaves of Grass

The Life Aquatic with Steve Zissou

Lock, Stock, and Two Smoking Barrels

London

Lords of Dogtown

Lost in Translation

Mallrats

Marihuana

Maryjane

Meet the Parents

Midnight Cowboy

Naked Lunch

National Lampoon's Animal House

National Lampoon's Totally Baked: A Potumentary

Natural Born Killers

Next Day Air

Next Friday

The Nine Lives of Fritz the Cat

One Flew Over the Cuckoo's Nest

Orange County

Outside Providence

Peace, Love, and Misunderstanding

The Perks of Being a Wallflower

PCU

Pineapple Express

Pink Floyd: The Wall

Pot Luck

Psych-Out

Puff, Puff, Pass

Pulp Fiction

Ray

Reefer Madness

Road Trip

Rock Opera

Rockers

Run, Lola, Run

Saving Grace

A Scanner Darkly

Sixteen Candles

Smiley Face

The Social Network

Stone & Ed

The Stoned Age

Stripes

Super High Me

Super Troopers

Superbad

Tenacious D in the Pick of Destiny

Things Are Tough All Over

Thirteen

This Is Spinal Tap

Tommy Boy

Training Day

Trainspotting

The Trip

True Romance

Twelve

The Union

A Very Brady Sequel

The Wackness

Water

Where the Buffalo Roam

Yellowbeard

Youth in Revolt

Zombieland

Medical Marijuana

The only thing left to say about the propaganda term "Reefer Madness," is that it is madness that reefer is not a staple of the American medical program by now.

Because all the lies and propaganda from the corporate-political conservative cadre to aimed at keeping marijuana illegal have been soundly disproven by science and medical research (not to mention by thousands of years of global empirical data), and we're not talking about alternative practitioners; we're talking about the most respected science and medical institutions on the planet.

Before the Marijuana Tax Act of 1937 passed, cannabis was the number-one prescribed medicine in the United States.

The fact is, cannabis is not only the most effective drug to treat the nasty symptoms of many diseases and pains, but in many cases, it's the only choice for patients. Cannabis is one-hundred percent natural, it has no debilitating side effects, it is not addictive, it is impossible to overdose, and it has been the most widely used drug on Earth for all of history, with positive writings on the topic from cultures in every corner of the globe across the centuries.

The only reason it's still illegal in the United States is because of corporate greed and corrupt politicians. Don't listen to any other "reason" coming from the politicians, the drug czars, the puritans, the paranoid, and even President Obama. They're all either lying or willfully ignorant. Their one goal is to serve their master, the almighty dollar, via the Big Pharmaceuticals whose multi-billion-dollar bottom line—gained by pushing shitty synthetic drugs with side-effects that are often worse than the pains they're meant to treat—would be destroyed in competition with legal medical marijuana, which can be grown by anyone for free. Get the picture?

What Is Medical Marijuana?

There's almost no difference between so-called "medical marijuana" and ganja or grass or weed or pot or any other name for recreational marijuana purchased illegally. The only reason we have the term "medical marijuana" is to separate it—politically—from recreational use, because everyone fighting to help patients ASAP realizes that it's still easier, politically, to try to legalize marijuana for medical reasons than for recreation.

The one slight difference is that medical marijuana has better quality control than "street weed" or anything you might buy from someone you don't really know. It's grown under state-approved guidelines, and its sale is regulated by strict rules.

But despite some political gains, medical marijuana is still not easy to come by. Only eighteen U.S. states have passed laws legalizing medical marijuana since 1996, and many medical-marijuana patients in those states can't even get to a legal dispensary and must buy it illegally from a dealer or other source. Also, federal laws still make marijuana illegal for any use, including state-sanctioned medical use, and the feds can and do continue to disrupt sick patients' healing by raiding medical-marijuana dispensaries that are operating legally under state laws.

What Does Medical Marijuana Do?

There's plenty of information available now about the specific health benefits of marijuana—from writings around the globe over the centuries, to recent medical and scientific studies from major institutions all over the world. Scientists have defined the ways cannabinoid receptors work in the human brain, and have determined exactly how marijuana works with those receptors to generate all kinds of physical and emotional benefits.

The straight dope is that marijuana is incredibly effective in controlling the symptoms of many diseases, physical pains, and emotional or spiritual problems. And in many of the most common ailments, the benefits from by marijuana blow away the legal pharmaceutical options in terms of effectiveness, cost, and side effects.

ADD and ADHD

For many years, the medical community has treated ADD (Attention Deficit Disorder) and ADHD (Attention Deficit Hyperactivity Disorder) with manmade drugs like Ritalin, which has been controversial for its side effects like nausea, headaches, and nervousness. A recent study by the University of Southern California proved that marijuana is a more effective drug than Ritalin at controlling these diseases in adults, while having none of the negative side effects, and costing far less.

ALZHEIMER'S DISEASE

Researchers at the respected Scripps Institute in 2006 proved that THC in marijuana blocks the deposits in the brain that cause Alzheimer's.

ANXIETY

Marijuana basically melts away anxiety for many people who suffer from it. (So do pills like Xanax and Prozac and other manmade drugs, but they cost a lot more, are addictive, and can have negative side effects.) Marijuana has no side effects as it soothes nerves, promotes relaxation, and allows better sleep, improving overall quality of life on a daily basis and extending life on a long-term basis.

CANCER

Marijuana haters love to say that smoking pot causes cancer, so it should stay illegal. The facts—proven in studies by top research institutes—state just the opposite. Cigarette smoke causes cancer, for one reason, because the tobacco is radiated when burned. Marijuana is not radiated when burned. In fact, the American Association for Cancer Research has found that marijuana works to inhibit tumor growth in the brain, breasts, and lungs significantly. And for the millions of marijuana users who don't smoke pot but rather eat or vaporize it, the cancer issue is just completely off the table.

CROHN'S DISEASE

Marijuana is proven to help patients with this chronic inflammation of the intestines, by relieving or outright stopping symptoms including nausea, abdominal pain, and diarrhea.

GLAUCOMA

This disease is the one most commonly associated with medical marijuana, whose use is well documented to be the best treatment for this painful eye disease.

HIV/AIDS

Studies at Columbia University (2007), the University of California, San Diego (2008), and others showed that HIV/AIDS patients who used cannabis daily had improved appetites, reduced pain, better mood, and other clear medical benefits that improve quality of life without any negative side effects.

MIGRAINES

Another health issue that affects millions on a chronic basis, migraines are more than just a headache. For many sufferers, marijuana has proved to be the most effective treatment for handling the pain and severe nausea that come with migraines. California doctors have treated over 300,000 cases of migraines with medicinal marijuana since it was legalized in 1996, and since the conventional (high-profit) drugs just didn't cut it.

MULTIPLE SCLEROSIS

This debilitating disease that alters normal communication between nerve cells in the brain and spinal cord affects hundreds of thousands of people with painful symptoms from cognitive difficulties to muscle control. Marijuana's positive effects on MS patients are well known, and have been championed by TV host Montel Williams, who began smoking pot to treat his disease and found it to be by far the best medicine for the job.

PMS (PREMENSTRUAL SYNDROME)

More and more women are turning to marijuana to treat the painful cramps, general discomfort, and irritability that comes around each month.

Queen Victoria was prescribed marijuana for just this reason by her physician over a hundred years ago.

SEIZURES

Marijuana is a muscle relaxant and has "antispasmodic" qualities which have proven to be a very effective treatment of seizures. There are actually countless cases of people suffering from seizures that have only been able to function better through the use of marijuana.

SPIRITUAL HEALING

A majority of stoners now and through time—from Joe Schmo to world-class achievers—have stated that marijuana, like nothing else, can open the mind to new trains of thought that lead to understanding, empathy, insight, and spiritual healing. Neurologically speaking, the THC in marijuana binds to the brain's cannabinoid receptors and causes you to temporarily lose the pinpoint focus on the moment that dominates sober reality. So the brain on pot gives you a broader relation to what's going on around you, and opens the conscious and subconscious mind to a different way of thinking, literally. Many accomplished people have credited marijuana with opening their minds to new thoughts that led to great discoveries and creations in science, art, music, and most other fields. The same principle can help anyone have positive insights that lead to great changes in their own life.

The Future of Medical Marijuana

A lot of headway has been made since the first medical marijuana law passed in 1996—there are now eighteen states that legalized it, and other states are putting up bills and propositions to legalize it every election cycle. For the first time since its ban over seventy-five years ago, according to a Rasmussen Poll in 2012, a majority of Americans (56%) believe that marijuana should be legalized for all purposes, not just medical.

As of 2013, though, this is where we stand:

■ LEGALIZED MEDICAL MARIJUANA

Get It Legal

By Cheech & Chong

It's a beautiful flower, that gives us a power
Overcoome sickness and dispare
It can 'elp you with cancer
Give you the answer
How to deal with their mess, so be fair

(Refrain)
And get it legal
Get marijuana legal now
Let's get it legal
And I don't care how

Our jails are overflowing
Got people waiting to get in
There are more heads in jail than ever before
The drug laws are a national scene
(Refrain)

Bustin' folks in New York City
And not the evil bastards that they should
They're busting the dope smoking hippies
Along with their brothers and the others
   in the hood
(Refrain)

Got people dying mothers crying
Drug cops ruining lives everyday
They'll be kicking down doors, and acting
   like hours
and the only thing that we do is pray
(Refrain)

"Get it Legal" © Cheech Marin and Tommy Chong

SPOT THE
Differences 2

Hey man, sorry about that—we fucked up back on page 106 and put the same picture twice. This picture here has the six differences you're supposed to spot. Good luck, homie.

1. _____

2. _____

3. _____

4. _____

5. _____

6. _____

HIGH-KU

Every stoner should know a few marijuana-inspired haikus—that cool, ancient Japanese poetry form that celebrates nature in three lines of five, seven, and five syllables, respectively. Here are a few that we wrote for you. And we left a little space for you to write one, too.

A pile of green leaves
A piece of paper waiting
To be rolled and smoked

After the doobie
When I finally get up
The fridge is frightened

Mary Jane my love
Your hairs are red and purple
And orange with flame

My-Ku:

_____

_____

_____

Time to

WAVE

and

BRAVE

Hang
"THE MAN"

Stoners love to play games, and here is one of the all-time classics—Hangman—with a little twist.

If you don't already know the game, here are the rules:

❊ You need two people to play—the Executioner and the Hangee.

❊ The Executioner starts by turning to page 156 to see the solution.

❊ The Hangee then starts guessing letters to try to form the solution words based on the blank spaces in the answer.

❊ For every wrong guess by the Hangee, the Executioner draws in another piece of the Hangee's stick-figure on the gallows, in this order—head, torso, right arm, left arm, right leg, left leg.

❊ If the Hangee gets the answer right before the last piece of body is drawn, they get to toke another day.

ANSWER: __ ___ __ . ___ ___ __ ___ __ ___ __

DOODLE TIME

Take a toke, pick a pen, and doodle down. The theme for this page is . . .

Freestyling

Solution to Hang "the Man": SGT. STEDENKO

~ 156 ~

Hazy Maze

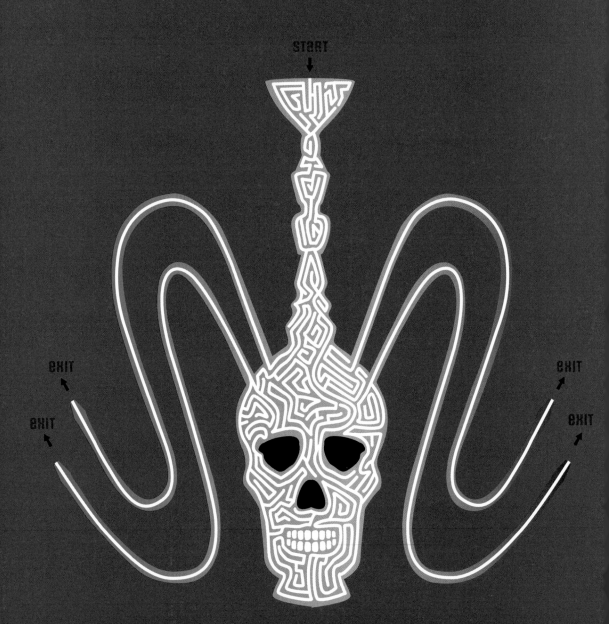

SMOKING TRICKS

It's good to know at least one smoke trick.
But it's a damn good time trying to learn them all.

SHOTGUN

The shotgun is an intimate and dangerous little number. It takes two to do it. The first person carefully places the lit end of a joint in their mouth and presses their lips closed near the unlit end sticking out. The second person opens their mouth and moves forward until their mouths are almost touching, and the first person blows into the joint, pushing smoke out into the open mouth.

SNAP INHALE

Fill your mouth with smoke and curl your tongue up behind your top teeth. Open your mouth just to show the smoke, then snap your tongue down and let a little smoke float out, and then inhale it. Looks different every time.

MOUTH-NOSE EXHALE

Take a big hit and inhale the smoke into your lungs, then exhale in short puffs alternating from your mouth to your nose until all the smoke is gone.

GHOST

Take a hit and let it sit inside your cheeks for a few seconds. Keep your lips puckered and your cheeks sucked in, then open your lips into a small O and gently pop out a tiny puff, backing away from it slightly. When the small ball of smoke pops out and hovers in front of you like a ghost, move forward and suck it all back into your mouth.

SMOKE RINGS

This is the trick everyone wants to learn, but it takes a lot of practice to get it down. Take a good-sized hit and keep it all in your mouth. Tilt your head back slightly, retract your tongue to the bottom of your mouth, open your lips in an O, then jab your tongue and lower-jaw forward to push out a small amount of smoke at a time. The puff should immediately form into a circle and float up into the air keeping its form. We suggest never doing more than one or two rings—the rest of that smoke in your mouth belongs in your lungs.

FRENCH INHALE

Also called the Irish Waterfall. Start with a nice big hit, but don't inhale—leave it in your mouth. Open your mouth and let the smoke flow out and up slowly, then breathe it back into your nostrils, and once all the smoke has gone from your mouth into your nostrils, blow it all out your mouth again.

CLOUD

Also known as Mushroom Cloud. With a mouthful of smoke, curl your lips and let it out slowly and consistently so it forms a cloud shape in the air, then suck it all back in.

INVISIBLE HIT

Take a big rip and hold it in for so long that, when you exhale, no smoke comes out. Virtually impossible, and not recommended.

SEEK & FIND

*Stoners often seem to be looking for something—the lighter,
their car keys, more weed, etc. See how many essentials
you can find in the grid below.*

```
Z  B  D  S  Y  P  K  B  E  L
D  R  E  M  O  T  E  K  L  H
A  T  A  L  E  V  B  T  D  I
Y  R  L  W  C  J  O  I  N  T
Q  F  E  B  A  M  R  D  E  P
E  C  R  T  S  N  D  I  I  S
X  A  F  C  H  O  S  H  R  W
A  R  I  M  O  G  V  W  F  E
W  X  Y  F  F  V  I  K  G  E
S  Y  E  K  G  R  O  L  B  D
```

Car	Friend	Remote
Cash	Joint	Weed
Dealer	Keys	
Food	Lighter	

Your Image Here

STONER

You know who you are.

STONER SLANG

Like any subculture, stoners have come up with all kinds of new words and slang terms for the cannabis plant, the people who enjoy it, the things they use to enjoy it with, and other miscellaneous items and concepts and whatnots.

The first list below includes lots of the different nicknames for weed—and as long as this list is, we probably left a few out.

The second list has everything else in stoner slang that we could think of, including the kitchen sink (see Gravity Bong).

Weed Words

420 * ACE * AFRICAN * Airplane * Angola * ASTROTURF * AUNT MARY * Bag * Baggie * BALES * BAMBA * Banana Leaves * BC Bud * BHANG * BLUNT * Bo * BOBO * BONE * Boo * Bricks * BROCCOLI * BUD * Buddha * Bush * BUTTER * BUZZ * Catnip * Cheeba * CHIEF * CHRISTMAS TREE * Chronic * Crippie * DAGGA * DANK * Devil's Lettuce * Devilweed * DIGGY * DIRTWEED * Ditchweed * Dobie * DON JUAN * DON JUANITA * Doob * Doobie * DOPE * DRAF * Earth * Finger * FIR * FIREWOOD * Flowers * Fuel * GAGE * GANJA * Gash * Gasper * GHANA * GIGGLE TWIG * Gold * Gong * GOODY-GOODY * GRAM * Grass * Green * GREENBUD * GREEN-STICKY * Griffa * Happy Backy * HASH * HASHISH * Hawaiian * Hay * HEMP * HERB * Hocus * Homegrown * HOOCH * HOOTER * Hops * Humboldt * HYDRO * INDO * Intsangu * J * Jane * JIVE * JOINT * Jolly Green * Joy Stick * JUAN VALDEZ * JUANITA * Juja * Justice * KAFF * KATE BUSH * Kaya * Keef * KEY * KIFF * Killer * Kilos * KIND BUD (OR KB) * KRYPTONITE * Kush * Laughing Grass * LEAF * LOAF * Lobo * Loco Weed * LOG * MARI * Marijuana * Mary Ann * MARY JANE * MEG * Method * Mexican * M.J. * MO * Moota * Mooters * MOOTIE * MOR A GRIFA * Mountain Cabbage * Muggle * NATURE'S HOLIDAY * NUBS * Nugs * Nuggets * NUGGIES * NUMBER * O.J. * Owl * PANAMA RED * PARSLEY * Philly Blunt * Pot * POUNDS * PRETENDICA * Puna Butter * Queen Ann's Lace * RAGWEED * RAINY DAY WOMAN * Rasta * Red Bud * RED CROSS

REEFER ✳ Rip ✳ Roach ✳ ROCKET ✳ ROOT ✳ Rope ✳ Scooby Doo ✳ SHIT ✳ SHWAG ✳ Skunk ✳ Smoke ✳ SNOP ✳ SPLIFF ✳ Stack ✳ Star ✳ STASH ✳ STICK ✳ Sticky Icky ✳ Stuff ✳ SWAZI ✳ SWEET LUCY ✳ Sweet Wheat ✳ Tea ✳ THAI-STICK ✳ THIRTEEN ✳ Thumb ✳ Tree of Wisdom ✳ TREES ✳ TURKISH DELIGHT ✳ Twigs ✳ WEED ✳ WHACKY TABACKY ✳ Whacky Weed ✳ Wheat ✳ WOOD ✳ YELLOW SUB-MARINE ✳ Yesca ✳ Zol

A Glossary

#

420: The magic number for stoners, it relates to 4:20 p.m. (a popular time for stoners to get high), and 4/20 or April 20 (the international feast day of cannabis); originated in 1971 among a group of San Rafael, CA, high school friends

A

Abe: Five dollars' worth of weed (about one small bud these days!)

Airhead: Someone who smokes weed

Airplane: A joint

Alice B. Toklas: Another name for hash brownies

All-American Smokeout: Getting together with friends to smoke a lot of weed

"Anything going on?": A sly way of asking if someone has marijuana to sell

"Are you anywhere?": A sly way to ask someone if they are a stoner

B

Baba Ku: Legendary Asian guy who turned Afghanistan on to hashish

Babysit: What you may have to do with a friend who is trying weed for the first time

Bag: A sandwich baggie with weed in it

Bagboy: Someone who sells weed for someone else

Bake a cake: Get stoned

Baked: Really stoned

Baker: Someone who deals or smokes marijuana

Bammy: Poor-quality weed with a lower THC count

Banana: A joint that gets bent like the yellow fruit

Baseball Bat: A perfectly rolled joint

Bat (see also: Dugout; One-hitter): A small marijuana pipe in the shape of a cigarette that fits one hit's worth of weed

Bazooka: To smoke weed

Beans: Seeds

Bhang: An Indian mixture of marijuana leaf resin and ghee butter

Binky: A joint

Black hash: Black-colored compressed kief from the Middle East

Blast: Smoke marijuana

Blaze: Smoke marijuana

Blazed: Blazingly stoned

Blond hash: Lighter color and usually mellower than black hash

Blow: Smoke marijuana

Blunt: Marijuana rolled in a tobacco leaf

Bob: A marijuana spliff

Bogart: Holding the joint or pipe too long when smoking with others

Bomb squad: Get together with friends to smoke up

Bomber: Fat joint

Bone: Joint

Bong: Water pipe

Bowling: Smoking pot out of a bowl

Brewery: A place where marijuana is grown

B.T.: Bong toke

Bud: A tightly compressed nugget of marijuana leaves

Buggin' out: Acting paranoid

Burning logs: Smoking joints

Burn one: Smoke a joint

Burnout: Someone who smokes too much weed

Burnt: Wasted

Burnt out: Unable to smoke pot anymore

Buzz: A nice little high

Buzzkill: Some negative person or thing or action that instantly makes you sober

C

Cadillac: An extra-long joint

Cake: Code word for marijuana

Cannabinoids (see also: THC): The special chemical compounds found in marijuana (and also found naturally in the human body, and in synthetic concoctions) that, when released into the body, create the feeling of euphoria known as being "high"

Canoe: When the joint starts to burn unevenly along one side

Cashed: The bowl or joint is out of weed

Cereal: Marijuana smoked out of a bowl

Cherry: Still-burning coal of weed in your joint or bowl

Chiefing: To smoke weed

Chillun: A type of pipe used to smoke weed

Chippie: A part-time stoner

Chronic: Killer bud

Chronnoisseur: Someone who knows their shit when it comes to marijuana strains

Clambake: Smoking marijuana in a small, enclosed space

Cloud: The smoke that fills the air after you exhale a large hit

Cola: Top bud on a marijuana plant

Commercial: Low-grade weed

Cone: A joint in the eponymous shape

Connoisseur: Marijuana aficionado and snob

Copping zone: An area where it's easy to buy marijuana

Cornering: Placing the fire on one side of the bowl, to leave fresh weed on the other side for the next toker

Cottonmouth: The dry-mouth effect of getting high

Creeperbud: Marijuana whose strong effects creep up on you

Cripple: A joint

Crunk: Being high and drunk at the same time

D

Daddy: A joint

Dank: Really good weed

Dealer: Your weed supplier

Dime: $1/16$ of an ounce of marijuana

Dime bag: $10 bag of weed

Dirt weed: Shitty marijuana

Ditch weed: Shitty marijuana

DL: Keep it on the Down Low

Dollar: $100 bag of weed

Doobie: A joint

Dope fiend: A constantly stoned person

Dry: Got no weed

Dub: $20 bag of weed (usually a gram)

Dugout (see also: Bat; One-hitter): A container that holds weed and a bat (a.k.a. one-hitter) for smoking out of

E

Egg: $1/8$ of an ounce of grass

Eight ball: $1/8$ of an ounce of marijuana

Eighth: $1/8$ of an ounce of pot

Elbow: One pound of marijuana

F

Fatty: (See: Phatty)

Fire one up: Light a joint

Fly Mexican Airlines: Slang for smoking marijuana

Flying: Very high

Fried: Really stoned

Frosted: Incredibly wasted

G

Ganja: Weed in Jamaica

Geeked out: Completely stoned

Get high: Smoke marijuana

Ghengis Chron: The best shit you ever smoked

Go loco: Smoke weed

Gone: Really, really stoned

Goose egg: One ounce of marijuana

Gravity bong: A powerful homemade bong using a bottle and container of water (like the kitchen sink)

Gurge: The dirty brown liquid at the bottom of a bong

H

Half: ½ ounce of marijuana

Harsh: When smoke is hot and hard on your throat

Hash, hashish: Condensed marijuana resin

Head Shop: A store that sells marijuana paraphernalia

Heater: The burning red end of a joint

Hemp: Non-psychoactive plant, related to *cannabis sativa*, that's used for many industrial purposes

Herb and Al: Marijuana and alcohol

High: Pleasant, euphoric feeling caused by THC

Hit: A drag of a joint, bowl, or bong

Hit the Hay: Smoke weed

Holding: In possession of marijuana

Hookah: Middle Eastern pipe with party hoses, originally for smoking flavored tobacco

Hooking up: Meeting a dealer somewhere to buy weed

Hot box: Smoking in a confined space, like inside a '57 Chevy

Hot rocks: The red-hot embers that fall off the tip of a joint

Hydro: Short for "hydroponic"— marijuana grown in water, not soil

I

Indica: One of two classes of cannabis (sativa is the other), with wider leaves and shorter plant height

In: A connection to a dealer

J

Johnny Law: A policeman

Joint (also, J): Marijuana rolled up in a rolling paper

Jonesing: Strong urge to score marijuana

K

KGB: Killer green bud

Kicked: So high that you're passed out

Kief: Crystals and powder from quality buds that's sprinkled on joints or bowlfuls

Kilo: 2.2 pounds of marijuana

Kind Bud: High-quality weed

Kram: Pack a tight bowl

Kron: See "Chronic"

L

Laced: When a marijuana joint has a more potent drug added to it

Lid: Pre-1990s: ¼ ounce of marijuana; Post-1990s: one ounce of weed

Lit up: High

Light up: To spark a joint or pipe or bong in order to get high

Lumber: Stems and other useless by-products of marijuana

M

Marijuana (or Marihuana): A Mexican slang term that was used by anti-weed propagandists in the U.S. in the 1930s that started the "Reefer Madness" movement to create a negative attitude toward the plant for political purposes and financial gain for a few pig industrialists

Milked: A bong filled with so much smoke that it looks like milk

Monty Hall: A weed buyer who always asks for a better deal

Mooch: Someone who loves sharing other people's stuff, but never offers their own

Mow the Grass: Smoke pot

Muggles: Slang for marijuana circa 1930s

Munchies: Relentless food cravings and gorgings

N

Nature's Holiday: Getting high; being high

Nickel bag: $5 bag of pot

NORML: National Organization for the Reform of Marijuana Laws

Nuggets or Nugs: Buds of weed

Number: Slang for a joint

O

One-hitter (see also: Bat; Dugout): A small marijuana pipe in the size/shape of a cigarette that fits one hit's worth of weed

Organic: Grown without pesticides and chemicals

O: One ounce of marijuana

O.Z.: One ounce of marijuana

Ozzie: One ounce of marijuana

P

Papers: Rolling papers

Pee a Bee: Pack a bowl

Permafried: Constantly high

Permasmile: The permanent smile on your face while high

Phatty: A big, thick joint

Piece: One ounce of marijuana

Pinner: A very thin joint

Pothead: A stoner

Pregnant: A poorly rolled joint due to the bump in the middle

Puff the Magic Dragon: Pot; smoking pot

Q

Q.P.: ¼ pound of marijuana

Quarter: ¼ ounce of marijuana

R

Ragweed: Poor-quality marijuana

Red-eye: Red, half-closed eyes resulting from smoking grass

Reeks: A strong, unmistakable smell of weed

Reggie: Regular weed

Resin: Residue from smoking that forms inside a bowl or bong and can be scraped and smoked

Rippie: Mash-up of the words "Republican" and "hippie" referring to a conservative-looking person who smokes weed

Roach: The small remains of a smoked joint

Roasted: High

S

Sativa: One of two classes of cannabis (indica is the other), with thinner leaves and taller plant height

Schwag: Shit weed

Score: Making a successful weed purchase

Screaming eagle: Sucking in a lit roach or a hot coal

Sensimilla: Seedless marijuana

Session (or Sesh): Getting together with friends to smoke pot

Shake: All the leftover leaves and bud fragments at the end of the bag

Shotgun: Inhaling marijuana smoke that's blown from another stoner's exhale

Sinsemilla: Seedless weed

Sketchy: A paranoid sensation that can sometimes result from getting high

Skin: A rolling paper

Smoke 'n' stroke: An adult bookstore that also sells marijuana paraphernalia

Smoke me out: Get me high

Spark it up: Get high

Spliff: Big cone-shaped joint in Jamaica

Sploof: A homemade device to exhale pot smoke into to destroy odor; usually made of a plastic bottle with no bottom, or an empty toilet-paper cardboard roll, filled with scented dryer sheets

Stash: Any place you store your weed

Stoner: Someone who smokes weed regularly

Stoned: High

Stupid: So high that you can't do anything

Straight: Someone who does not smoke weed

T

Tea head: Regular marijuana smoker

Tea party: Gathering with friends to smoke pot

THC: Tetrahydrocannabinol, the psychoactive ingredient in marijuana

Toasted: High

Toke: Take a hit from a bong, joint, or pipe

Toothpick: A tightly rolled, thin joint

Torch: Lighter

Trichomes: Tiny crystals on leaves and buds of the marijuana plant

Twenty and forty: A $20 bag of weed and a 40-ounce bottle of beer

Twist one up: Roll a joint

Toke choke: Holding your hit in until the joint is passed around the circle

U

Uncle Bob: Code for smoking weed (reference to Bob Marley)

V

Vape: Short version of "vaporizer"

Vaporizer: A device that heats marijuana so it does not burn but does release THC; it's healthier than smoking, produces the same high, and requires less weed than burning

Viper: A stoner, circa 1930s (a reference to the snake's "Sssssst" sound of drawing in a hit from a joint)

W

Wake and Bake: Getting high first thing in the morning

Wasted: Completely high

Weed whacked: Somehow prevented from doing a planned smoking session

Wizard of Oz: One ounce of marijuana

Wishbone: An extra-large joint (i.e. "I wish every bone was that size.")

wXc: Online tag that tells others you are a stoner, in code

X

X-ray eyed: Stoned to the point you can barely see straight

Z

Z: One ounce

Zip: One ounce

Zone: One ounce

weed sites

You can spend hours online going from one great weed site to another, and you probably do. Check out these few sites to start with for both real info and fun and games.

@cheechmarin

@tommychong

420girls.com

420magazine.com

amsterdammarijuanaseedbank.com

cannabisculture.com

celebstoner.com

cheechandchong.com

davesnothereman.com

drchronic.com

freemarc.ca

friendsofcannabis.com

grasscity.com

hailmaryjane.com

highdeas.com

highroulette.com

hightimes.com

icmag.com
(International Cannagraphic)

iloveweed.net

jackherer.com

joerogan.net

justgethigh.com

legalmarijuanadispensary.com

mapinc.org
(Media Awareness Project)

marijuanaseedbanks.com

marijuana-seeds.nl

medicalmarijuanablog.com

mpp.org
(Marijuana Policy Project)

norml.org

pixel.org.ua

planetskunk.com

progressivegatherings.com

reefersmoke.com

rollitup.org

roor.de

saferchoice.org

seedboutique.com

smokingwithstyle.com

stonerforums.com

stonersunited.com

thcfinder.com

the420times.com

thechronic-le.blogspot.com

thefreshscent.com

thestonerscookbook.com

tokecity.com

tokeofthetown.com

veryimportantpotheads.com

weedfarmer.com

weed-forums.com

wearebaked.com

Changin' Books

Everything is more fun when you know more about it. If you're starting a pot library, here are a few titles you might want to score for your shelves for starters.

10% THC, A Cannabis Tale, Frank William "Eagle Bill" Wood

The Benefits of Marijuana: Physical, Psychological and Spiritual, Joan Bello

The Big Book of Buds, Ed Rosenthal

The Botany of Desire: A Plant's-Eye View of the World, Michael Pollan

Budding Prospects: A Pastoral, T. Coraghessan Boyle

Build This Bong, Randy Stratton

The Cannabible, Jason King

Cannabis: A History, Martin Booth

Cannabis Alchemy: Art of Modern Hashmaking, D. Gold

The Cannabis Breeder's Bible: The Definitive Guide to Marijuana Genetics, Cannabis Botany and Creating Strains for the Seed Market, Greg Green

The Cannabis Companion, Steven Wishnia

The Cannabis Cookbook, Tim Pilcher

Cannabis Cultivation: A Complete Grower's Guide, Mel Thomas

The Cannabis Grow Bible: The Definitive Guide to Growing Marijuana for Recreational and Medical Use, Greg Green

Cannabis—Philosophy for Everyone: What Were We Just Talking About, Fritz Allhoff

Cannabis Trips, Bill Weinberg

Cheech & Chong: The Unauthorized Autobiography, Thomas Chong

Cooking with Cannabis: The Most Effective Methods of Preparing Food and Drink with Marijuana, Hashish, and Hash Oil, Adam Gottlieb

Cultivating Exceptional Cannabis: An Expert Breeder Shares His Secrets (Marijuana Tips Series), DJ Short

Dank: the Quest for the Very Best Marijuana: A Breeder's Tale, Subcool

The Emperor Wears No Clothes: The Authoritative Historical Record of Cannabis and the Conspiracy Against Marijuana, Jack Herer

The Great Books of Cannabis, Book II, Laurence Cherniak

The Great Books of Hashish, Book 3 (The Great Books of Hashish 1st Trilogy), Laurence Cherniak

Grow Great Marijuana: An Uncomplicated Guide to Growing the World's Finest Cannabis, Logan Edwards

Hashish, Robert Connell Clarke

The I Chong: Meditations from the Joint, Thomas Chong

The Little Black Book of Marijuana: The Essential Guide to the World of Cannabis, Steve Elliot

Marihuana: The Forbidden Medicine, Lester Grinspoon

Marijuana Botany: An Advanced Study: The Propagation and Breeding of Distinctive Cannabis, Robert Connell Clarke

Marijuana Garden Saver: Handbook for Healthy Plants, J. C. Stitch

Marijuana Grow Basics: The Easy Guide for Cannabis Aficionados, Jorge Cervantes

Marijuana Grower's Handbook: Your Complete Guide for Medical and Personal Marijuana Cultivation, Ed Rosenthal

Marijuana Horticulture: The Indoor/Outdoor Medical Grower's Bible, Jorge Cervantes

Marijuana Indoors: Five Easy Gardens, Jorge Cervantes

Marijuana Is Safer: So Why Are We Driving People to Drink?, Steve Fox

The Marijuana-logues: Everything About Pot That We Could Remember, Arj Barker

Marijuana Medical Handbook: Practical Guide to Therapeutic Uses of Marijuana, Dale H. Gieringer

Marijuana Myths Marijuana Facts: A Review Of The Scientific Evidence, Lynn Zimmer

Marijuana Reconsidered, Lester Grinspoon

Medical Marijuana Handbook, Dale Gieringer and Ed Rosenthal

The Official High Times Field Guide to Marijuana Strains, Danny Danko

The Official High Times Pot Smokers Handbook, David Bienenstock

The Pot Book: A Complete Guide to Cannabis, Julie Holland M.D.

Pot Culture: The A-Z Guide to Stoner Language and Life, Steve Bloom

Red-Dirt Marijuana and Other Tastes, by Terry Southern

Reefer Madness: A History of Marijuana, Larry Sloman

Reefer Movie Madness: The Ultimate Stoner Film Guide, Steve Bloom

The Science of Marijuana, Leslie L. Iversen

Shattered Lives: Portraits from America's Drug War, Mikki Norris

Spliffigami: Roll the 35 Greatest Joints of All Time, Chris Stone

Spliffs: A Celebration of Cannabis Culture, Nick Jones

Understanding Marijuana: A New Look at the Scientific Evidence, Mitchell Earleywine

Weed: 420 Things You Didn't Know (or Remember) about Cannabis, I.M. Stoned

PHOTO/ART CREDITS

t= top, b = bottom, c = center, l = left, r = right

Illustrations by Susan Van Horn: 1 & 3 (marijuana leaves), 11, 27 (seated figure), 44–45, 62, 64 tr, 71, 74, 87, 92, 95, 97, 100, 101, 120–126, 130–131, 156, 158–159, 162

Front cover: LEmir/Shutterstock.com (smoke); ©iStockphoto.com/stereohype (line illustration in "Stoners")

1: Up in Smoke © Paramount Pictures. All Rights Reserved. Photo Courtesy of Everett Collection.

1, 3: ©iStockphoto.com/stereohype (line illustration in "Stoners")

4: LEmir/Shutterstock.com

5: Michael Bezjian/WireImage/Getty Images

6: ©iStockphoto.com/stereohype

9: ©Accent Alaska.com/Alamy (joint)

9 tl: Michael Putland/Hulton Archive/ Getty Images

9 tr: ©ImageCollect.com/Globe-Photos

9 b: AP Images/Krista Kennell/Sipa Press

9: ©iStockphoto.com/PhotoGraphyKM (loose marijuana)

10: ©iStockphoto.com/John Woodcock

12: V&A Images, London/Art Resource, NY

13: Mary Evans/Everett Collection

14 l: The Art Archive/SuperStock

14 r: ©Science Museum/SSPL/The Image Works

15 l: Axiom Photographic/Design Pics/ SuperStock

15 r: AP Images/Ted S. Warren

16–17: ©iStockphoto.com/simonox (car)

17: ©iStockphoto.com/Cabezonication (marijuana bud on bumper stickers); ©iStockphoto.com/Nemanja Pesic (baggie on bumper sticker)

18 t: ©iStockphoto.com/Cabezonication

18 b: AP Images/Allen Green

21, 25, 108, 109, 151: Craig Joiner/age fotostock/SuperStock

22: Stellar Stock/SuperStock

23: KR MEDIA Productions/Shutterstock.com

26 t: SuperStock; Susan Van Horn (frame)

26 bl: Michael Ochs Archives/Getty Images

26 br: ©iStockphoto.com/Debbi Smirnoff

27 br: ©iStockphoto.com/101cats

27 t: ©iStockphoto.com/billnoll (spiral motifs)

28: Courtesy Everett Collection

30 l & r: Everett Collection/SuperStock

32: ©iStockphoto.com/Nemanja Pesic

34 tr: AP Images/CP, Richard Lam

34 bl: Matthew Staver/Landov

34 br: ©ImageCollect.com/Graham Whitby Boot-allstar-Globe Photos, Inc.

35 t: Reuters/Tim Wimborne/Landov

35 l: ©ImageCollect.com/Henry Mcgee-Globe Photos, Inc. 2012.

35 r: AP Images/Stephen Chernin

36 t: AP Images/Marcio Jose Sanchez

36–37: Logos Courtesy of Americans for Safe Access (ASA), High Times,

Marijuana Policy Project (MPP), National Organization for the Reform of Marijuana Laws (NORML), Students for Sensible Drug Policy (SSDP)

38–39: ©iStockphoto.com/julioechandia

40: Marka/SuperStock

41 l: Photoshot/Everett Collection

41 r: Ray Tamarra/Everett Collection

42 t & b: Courtesy Everett Collection

43 t: ©ImageCollect.com/Lane Ericcson-PHOTOlink.net

43 b: Visual & Written/SuperStock

46: Jared Shomo/Shutterstock.com (clock)

46: ©iStockphoto.com/ihor_seamless (border around clock)

48: AP Images/The Canadian Press, Darryl Dyck

49: viphotos/Shutterstock.com

50: MGP, Inc./Science Faction/SuperStock

51 t: ©ImageCollect.com/ GTCRFOTO

51 b: AP Images/Keith Srakocic

52: Photo by Dezo Hoffmann/ Rex USA, Courtesy Everett Collection

53 t: CSU Archives/Everett Collection

53 b: Courtesy Everett Collection

54: Photo By Brian Rasic/Rex Features/Courtesy Everett Collection

55: Richard E. Aaron/Redferns/Getty Images

56: Mark Grenier/Shutterstock.com

57: ©iStockphoto.com/Favna

62 tl: Portokalis/Shutterstock.com

62 bl: Benno Friedman//Time Life Pictures/Getty Images

62 br: iStockphoto/Thinkstock

61–62 c: Steve Cukrov/Shutterstock.com

63 t: ©ImageCollect.com/Nate Cutler / Globe Photos, Inc.

63 b: Brand X Pictures/Thinkstock

64 l: ©iStockphoto.com/mirkamoksha

64 r: ©iStockphoto.com/Ivan Ivanov

65: ©ZUMA Press, Inc./Alamy

67: ©Premierlight Images/Alamy

68: Richard E. Aaron/Redferns/Getty Images

71: ©EGimages/Alamy

75: Cindy Shebley/Shutterstock.com (lunchbox)

75: ©eddie linssen/Alamy (lighter, tin & joints)

75: ©Accent Alaska.com/Alamy (pipe, pot & rolling paper)

76–77: ©iStockphoto.com/Denise Bush

78 tl: AP Images/Armando Franca

78 bl: AP Images/Ann Arbor News, Leisa Thompson

78 r: AP Images/Peter Dejong

81 l: ©Peter Ptschelinzew/Alamy

81 tr: ©ZUMA Press, Inc./Alamy

81 br: ©iStockphoto.com/Douglas Rial

82 tl: Brian Weed /Shutterstock.com

82 tr: K13 ART /Shutterstock.com

82 bl: Fotosearch

82 br: Yurchyks/Shutterstock.com

83 l: Aptyp_koK/Shutterstock.com

83 r: hangtime/Shutterstock.com

84: Courtesy of The VaporBLUNT

86: Flirt/SuperStock

89: Photo by Waring Abbott/Michael Ochs Archives/Getty Images

94 tl: ©GanjaFoto/Alamy

94 cl: ©Hugh Threlfall/Alamy

94 bl: ©iStockphoto.com/leviticus

94 r: Up in Smoke © Paramount Pictures. All Rights Reserved. Photo Courtesy of Everett Collection.

101: age fotostock/SuperStock

102 tl: TOMO/Shutterstock.com

102 tc: Fotokostic/Shutterstock.com

102 tr: ©iStockphoto.com/Anneclaire Le Royer

102 bl: ©H. Mark Weidman Photography/Alamy

102 bc: Clover/SuperStock

102 br: ©Rick & Nora Bowers/Alamy

103 tl: ©Suzanne Long/Alamy

103 tc: watin/Shutterstock.com

103 tr: ©iStockphoto.com/Kelly Cline

103 cl: Ted Bodner @ USDA-NRCS PLANTS Database/ James H. Miller and Karl V. Miller. 2005

103 cc: Jumnong /Shutterstock.com

103 cr: Jody,/Shutterstock.com

103 bl: ©iStockphoto.com/Jivko Kazakov

103 bc: ©Ross Frid/Alamy

103 br: ©Arco Images GmbH/Alamy

105: ©iStockphoto.com/Luis Carlos Torres (chocolate); Amero/Shutterstock.com (donuts); Bryan Solomon/Shutterstock.com (tortilla chip); Valentyn Volkov/Shutterstock.com (hot dog); Ivaschenko Roman/Shutterstock.com (pickle); ©iStockphoto.com/Eldad Carin (joint)

108: Mark Grenier/Shutterstock.com

109: Sergiy Kubyk/Shutterstock.com (rubber duck); Susan Van Horn (marijuana leaf)

111: AP Images/Matt Sayles

113: ©iStockphoto.com/Chris Zawada

114: ©iStockphoto.com/Eldad Carin

116 bl: Ron Galella/WireImage/Getty Images

116–117: iStockphoto/Thinkstock (paint splatter, dart board)

116–117: IrinaK/Shutterstock.com (turtles)

117 t: Ed Caraeff/Michael Ochs Archive/Getty Images

117 b: ©iStockphoto.com/bpablo

125: ©ImageCollect.com/Rudy Rodriguez/Globe Photos

126 l: ©ImageCollect.com/Globe-Photos

126 c: AP Images/Alan Greth

126 r: ©ImageCollect.com/Globe-Photos

127 l: AP Images/Hubert Boesl/picture-alliance/dpa

127 r: AP Images/Adrian Sidney/PictureGroup

130–139: ©iStockphoto.com/Denise Bush (tie-dye backgrounds)

130: ©ImageCollect.com/Paul Fenton/Zumapress

131: ©ImageCollect.com/StarMax-Worldwide

132: Courtesy Everett Collection

133, 135: ©ImageCollect.com/S Bukley

134: ©ImageCollect.com/Jeff Spicer-alpha-Globe Photos

136: Photo By Jonathan Player/Rex Features/Courtesy Everett Collection

137: ©ImageCollect.com/Dave Gadd-Allstar-Globe Photos, Inc. 2008

138: ©ImageCollect.com/Mario Santoro/AdMedia

139: SuperStock

140: ©iStockphoto.com/Chris Rogers (NY skyline); 29september/Shutterstock.com (bong)

141: ©iStockphoto.com/gbrundin (bowling pins); andersphoto/Shutterstock.com (rose petals)

141 b: Up in Smoke © Paramount Pictures. All Rights Reserved.

141–143: ©iStockphoto.com/ihor_seamless (background illustration)

142: Arthur Dent/Shutterstock.com (feather); Steve Collender/Shutterstock.com (surfboard); ©iStockphoto.com/FredS (ground hog doll); ©iStockphoto.com/rjlerich (hamburgers); ©iStockphoto.com/Thinkstock (bottle)

143: Levent Konuk/Shutterstock.com (wool cap); Valentina Proskurina/Shutterstock.com (pineapple); Mike Flippo/Shutterstock.com (guitar)

144: Corbis/SuperStock

147: ©iStockphoto.com/appleuzr

148: John Shearer/WireImage/Getty Images

151: Marilyn Volan/Shutterstock.com

152–153: Pavel Vakhrurshev/Shutterstock.com

155: Mark Grenier/Shutterstock.com

158–159: ©iStockphoto.com/Elemental-Imaging (tie-dye swirl background); ©iStockphoto.com/Thinkstock (paisley illustration)

158-159: ©iStockphoto.com/Eldad Carin, Brian C. Weed /Shutterstock.com, and ©iStockphoto.com/Thinkstock (rolled joints)

162: ©iStockphoto.com/bgblue

176: ©iStockphoto.com/stereohype